❧ THE GARDEN ❧ COTTAGE DIARIES

"Done with great wit and intelligent determination . . .
A sane response in a relentlessly consuming
and resource-depleted world."
FELICITY LAWRENCE, THE GUARDIAN

"A riveting tale of a rather extraordinary journey"
FAMILY HISTORY MONTHLY

"A fascinating and colourful scrapbook . . . an
object of delight . . . If ever you needed an argument
for the survival of the printed book, this is it."
SALLY MACPHERSON, REFORESTING SCOTLAND JOURNAL

"I couldn't put it down."
SARAH PALMER, ORGANIC GARDEN AND HOME

To Rhona

❧ THE GARDEN ❧
COTTAGE DIARIES

My Year in the
Eighteenth Century

Best wishes

Fiona J. Houston

Saraband ◉

Saraband
Suite 202, 98 Woodlands Road
Glasgow, G3 6HB, Scotland
www.saraband.net

ISBN: 978-1-887354-77-6

Printed and bound in the EU on Amber Graphic (chlorine-free paper, FSC-certified, from mixed sources).

10   9   8   7   6   5   4   3   2   1

Scottish Arts Council The publisher acknowledges subsidy from the Scottish Arts Council towards the publication of this volume.

For A.M.
In memoriam

Editor: Sara Hunt
Designer: Deborah White
Copy editor: Clare Haworth-Maden
Editorial assistant: Sara Myers
Original artwork by Clare Melinsky (© 2009 Clare Melinsky)
Photography: see photo credits on page 221
Prepress support: Tegra Premedia

CONTENTS

A NOTE ON THE RECIPES. Many of the recipes in this book date from the eighteenth century. They employ a non-metric measuring system and frequently use rather rough quantities, a 'pinch of salt' or a 'handful of kail'. These arise naturally in households without scales, where girls would have learned to cook by watching and helping older women. Fortunately, the size of our hands hasn't changed much since the eighteenth century. Most recipes are forgiving and flexible, so use the following recipes as guidelines and experiment on your own.

WHEN GATHERING WILD FOOD - be sure that you can identify anything you pick from the wild; avoid polluted areas and wash it carefully before you consume it. Many edible flowers and plants look very similar to poisonous species, and the photos in this book are not a sufficient basis for identification. Never uproot wild plants or pick more than you will use, and never disturb wildlife or wild habitats.

Innerleithen, viewed from the route from my cottage

Scotland's national flower.

Two of my hens.

CHAPTER 1
"You Try it, Then!"

January 1st, 2005

The wind howled and shrieked, chasing away all night at the cottage. It was unsettling. I was too jumpy to get to sleep. The slates danced on the roof, the chimney roared, and my wool-stuffed mattress felt strange and lumpy. It was like being out at sea, in an unfamiliar berth. I was chilly, but somehow I finally dozed off. When I woke – I've no idea at what time – it was to absolute darkness. I am used to darkness, but the cottage windows are tiny. I had closed up the shutters on the field side, but the other window is around a corner. Whatever starlight there may have been between the wind-whipped clouds, it could not filter through to me in my closed box bed.

I N TIME, I learnt how to register the different nuances of grey that denote a cloudy night, a bright night, and the start of dawn. I learnt to slip out of bed in all but total darkness to pee in a bucket. But that night it was a challenge to place my feet on the kist below the box bed and lower myself to the floor. I stumbled to the fire and saw a tiny glow. Feeling that it was beyond me to find the log basket and feed it in the dark, I groped my way back to bed and huddled there, waiting for daylight.

What had brought me to this dark and chilly cottage? It is a story that stretches right back through my life. I don't romanticise the past, but it intrigues me. Since my earliest childhood, with my father and 'Uncle Arthur', a family friend whose passion for archaeology inspired us all, I have field-walked, looking for evidence of past habitation. I was brought up in Lincolnshire, where Roman roads scored their straight lines across the county and the Anglian people had left their mark, not just in place names but in cemeteries of burial urns, two of which I helped to excavate. This was formative stuff for a seven-year-old. It stirred up my interest in the people who had come before us. I was drawn to the sherds of old pottery that I so readily picked up. Together with the clay pipe stems from our vegetable garden, they formed my earliest collections. These simple domestic things, rather than the kings and queens of *A Child's Illustrated History of Britain*, fascinated me. I wondered about the daily lives of the people to whom they had belonged. What might life have been like for a native Iron Age woman in Roman Britain, or for the eighteenth-century gardener who had broken his pipe? So when I came to Scotland as an adult, it was natural for me to ask questions about the details of the daily lives of ordinary people in the centuries before the Industrial Revolution changed the face of the countryside forever.

To answer my own questions, I have spent years looking at ruined croft houses in the Highlands and sizing up any footings that I could find of the simple turf-and-stone houses that were common in the Lowlands before 1800. I have scoured junk shops for domestic relics. I have read books, studied drawings and paintings that give clues about house interiors, and I have spent many happy hours in museums.

This all prepared the ground for what I was toying with doing as an experiment. I was becoming more and more attracted to the idea of putting the clock back, and living as people might have done two hundred years ago. All that was needed was some extra impetus to tip me into getting on with it. Then, whilst researching the history of Scottish food for an exhibition in local museums, I read *Not on the Label* by Felicity Lawrence, food writer for

A tallow candle and one of beeswax, made in moulds that would have been illicit in the eighteenth century.

I became used to darkness, and welcomed a moonlit night.

The Guardian. Her shocking revelations about the machinations of supermarkets angered me so much that I started to relay them to anyone who would listen. Whatever they may tell their customers, supermarkets' sole interest is in selling products in order to give a good return to their shareholders. They do not care about the nutritional value of their food, about the environmental impact of their operation, or, most especially, about the survival of the poor people who actually farm the crops that end up, in one form or another, on supermarket shelves. Their whole operation is ethically suspect, the 'greenwash' handed out by their publicity departments.

My rant had gone on. It probably wasn't the first time that I had ranted, either. I was so focused on the unwholesomeness of lots of so-called 'food products': crisps, confectionary, sweet drinks, ready-made meals, that I was in danger of becoming a bore. I declared that people in Scotland were better fed at the end of the eighteenth century than they are now. Someone called my bluff. "You try living as they did in the eighteenth century!" he said.

So I decided I would.

Moreover, I decided to live that way for a whole calendar year. I did not want to dabble. I wanted to experience the realities of all seasons with their pleasures and hardships, to cut off from the industrialized world for a significant stretch of time.

How much more enjoyable, not to mention healthy, is a bowl of freshly picked berries than a sugary snack?

Alexander Carse's painting depicts a domestic scene around the end of the eighteenth century.

I had other motives, of course. By doing something so unusual, I knew that I had a good chance of having my story published in a newspaper. I saw this as being central to my endeavour. My pitch worked. I was given a monthly page in *The Herald*, originally the daily read for the west of Scotland, but increasingly for the entire country. I needed that audience because it would keep up my resolve. I also anticipated there being a good deal to say, not least because, in looking back to the simple life of the past, I had one eye on the future.

We none of us know what the next decades hold for us. The evidence is gathering fast that global warming is becoming a reality that will affect us here directly, and all too soon. Our weather is becoming more unpredictable and violent. In many more distant parts of the world, land is now liable to catastrophic flooding, or else is burning up and turning into deserts where no crops can be grown. Suddenly, life as we know it seems to be very much more precarious than before. Some authorities suggest that the whole biosphere is at risk; others foretell consequences that are almost as dire.

James Lovelock, the originator of the Gaia Hypothesis (which sees the Earth as acting almost as though it were a living organism), thinks that we have pushed carbon-dioxide levels too far already. He postulates that by 2045, the globe will support only one-tenth of its current population. His map of the world in 2045 shows a little band of habitable land around the south of the globe, including Tasmania and New Zealand, and another around the north. Scotland is embraced within his habitable zone.

I hadn't seen that map when I dreamt up my experiment. But I had considered how fragile contemporary lifestyles are. 'Peak Oil', the point at which consumption overtakes production, is either with us or very near at hand. Yet almost everything that we do is predicated on cheap fossil fuels. Local production, distribution and the purchase of local food and goods have all but disappeared. Remove the fossil fuels, or make it untenable to go on using them, and our life-support systems grind to a halt.

This would be an almost insurmountable disaster for the majority of the population, the city-dwellers, who have no options but to buy what they need. Even for people like me, who live in the country, life would be taxing. The subsistence economy has gone. Farmers may husband sheep and cattle, but very few of them provide directly for their own tables. The days when oats and barley were milled on the farm or at the local mill for consumption in the same parish have long gone. Even the practice of farms growing a few riggs (the old name has persisted) of tatties for their own use has almost disappeared. Fewer and fewer country people have vegetable gardens, even though the demand for urban allotments is going up and up.

Yet my house is an old manse, and it does have a vegetable garden. The Church used to provide well for its ministers, so although it is situated at 650 feet above sea-level, it is surrounded by a wall high enough to create something of a micro-climate. For more than twenty years, I have dug my vegetable garden, heaped on compost, spread dung donated by my farmer neighbours over it, and have harvested, in good years, enough to feed a family of four and a multitude of

The veggie garden I've nurtured for more than two decades now.

The byre that became my cottage for the year-long experiment.

visitors. So for my eighteenth-century experiment, I was confident that I could provide for myself, especially as there are now no other permanent residents in my home, just a shifting population of family and friends.

So that crucial element of my proposed plan felt secure. I also had a cottage near the house, or something resembling one. At the start of 2004, when I was hatching my idea about returning to the past, I stood in the byre that we used as a workshop and saw that it must once have been a lived-in cottage. Byres were never built with windows and a chimney. One of the windows was boarded up. The other was in need of a new frame. The door, which was ancient and bore initials of past incumbents of the manse, or their children, was admitting a howling gale. It would take some work, but I could see that it would do.

At that point, I remembered my ancestor, William Houston, a schoolmaster in Galloway during the 1790s. I no longer know the whereabouts of the family Bible that records the details, but I recollect that he married an English wife called Anne. I used to think about her when, English-reared, I came to Scotland and struggled to fit in with a different culture. How can it have been for her at the end of the eighteenth century, finding herself in a country where the houses were ruder and more dirty, material goods were scantier, and life was generally far harder than in England? How was her house furnished and equipped? Did anyone help her with tasks like laundry? Did she dig her own garden? If so, what did she wear on her feet?

It occurred to me that Anne and William and the everyday details of their lives, could become my benchmarks. They held exactly the right rank in society. A schoolmaster was given a house, a garden and a small stipend. This was often augmented with several bolls of oatmeal and barleymeal. A boll is 140 lb (about 64 kg), so I could feel free to order meal by the sack and would not have to worry about growing and harvesting field crops. In order to get the best out of her garden, the schoolmaster's wife would have had to be practical, a hands-on gardener. She would also, in all probability, have been literate. Both of those features made the prospect of using Anne as a model tenable.

The problem was that I knew nothing about her. I swithered about whether to try to recreate the life of a minister's wife instead, as that would be easier to research. But such a woman would have been an important figure in society. Her household would have been run by servants, and her employment would have been as much in the parish as at home. I did not want to try to take my real house too far back in time. This would have been too complicated and too costly. (Imagine taking out all of the wiring and other modern conveniences!) It would be simpler to opt for the unimproved cottage.

As the idea crystallised in my mind, a multitude of necessary practical tasks became evident. The cottage needed attention. The chimney was half-blocked with fallen masonry, as I discovered when I tried to light a fire in the tiny, low fireplace and smoke billowed back into the room, our old picture-framing workshop. The windows would clearly need to be replaced. Above all, the floor would have to be changed. It was cobbled and sloping, built so that the byre's floor would drain towards the door. I contemplated living on it, but only for a moment. House floors were not usually cobbled in the past, for a cobbled surface is too uneven, so when this building was actually lived in, I guessed that it would have had an earthen floor.

I left the cobbles on the floor of the outer room when I made the wooden floor for the main cottage room.

A 1790s Scottish 'improvement cottage'.

A table from the First Statistical Accounts showing figures for a day labourer's family.

	£	s.	d.
To 48 weeks' labour of a man at 1s. a day	14	8	0
To 48 weeks' labour of a woman, in spinning, besides taking care of her house and children	3	12	0
To the earnings of three children at the age of six, seven, and eight years	0	0	0
	£18	0	0

ANNUAL EXPENSES

	£	s.	d.
By 2 pecks oatmeal a week, at 1½d. per week	4	19	8
By 2 pecks barley or pease meal a week at 7½d.	3	5	0
By 6 bolls potatoes, at 5s. the boll	1	10	0
By barley for kail, at 3lb a week	0	16	3
By a kail-yard, and a wretched house		13	0
By milk, at 4d. a week		17	4
By salt, cheese and butter		12	6
By soap for washing clothes		2	6
By coals in a year, and carriage	1	0	0
By shoes to the whole family	1	0	0
By body clothes to the man	1	10	0
By ditto to the woman and children	1	5	0
By worsted thread for mendings		7	0
	£17	18	3

My guess was accurate. Before I organised the laying of joists and the running of a board floor over the cobbles, I did a little excavation. The 'habitation layer', as archaeologists would call it, was more than a foot below the cobbles and did consist of a well-beaten, earth floor. Again, I contemplated lifting the cobbles and using the older level of flooring, but I soon thought again. Commonplace as earth floors were in Scotland at the end of the eighteenth century, anyone with any ambition or social status would have aspired to get up off the dirt. These old floors were dusty in summer, and inevitably got muddy in winter, when wet feet tramped in. The fine, straight boards that estate sawmills were starting to turn out would have provided a most attractive alternative.

Would a dominie's house have had a wooden floor? That would have depended on the generosity, or otherwise, of the parish heritors. These were the landowners who were responsible for repairing the church, and contributing to both the minister's and dominie's stipend. I have no idea about the realities of the Galloway parish of my forebears, but I decided to make the assumption that my own parish was free with its money. Indeed, I had the evidence from the First Statistical Accounts that the heritors were busy paying for the building of a new manse here, the very house I now live in.

The First Statistical Accounts, a treasure chest of information, was another reason for my choosing the 1790s for my experiment. In around 1790, Sir John Sinclair of Caithness persuaded the government in Westminster that the king should have a record of his entire realm. He accordingly drew up a pro-forma, which was sent to every parish minister in Scotland. The plan was to extend the inquiry to England, although very few parishes there were actually recorded. But by 1794, almost all of the Scottish accounts had been returned, the volumes of records being published as they became available. The Accounts vary a little, according to the particular interests of the ministers, but all include information about farming, housing and how people earned a living. The best contain details of dress and even typical annual accounts for households. They make an invaluable resource for anyone delving into everyday lives of the period.

Beyond searching in that source, I was starting to look forward to reading diaries and other material relating to 'my' decade. On my shelves were travellers' accounts of Scotland: those by Thomas Pennant (which were published earlier, in 1769 and 1772), Dorothy Wordsworth's *Recollections of a Tour Made in Scotland* (published just a few years later), and *Memoirs of a Highland Lady*, by Elizabeth Grant of Rothiemurchus, which was also published later, but harked back to about 1803. I could see that I was setting myself up to learn a lot, but I did hope that I would have some fun. At the same time, I was apprehensive about lumbering myself with a great deal of tedium and drudgery.

What inspired me to press on with the plan was an abiding desire to try out life without modern communications and conveniences and all the pressures they inadvertently impose on us. I was eager to start the simple year.

Simple artefacts for a simple year. But how would I get on when it became a reality?

∿ CHAPTER 2 ∿
Setting Up

THE COTTAGE THAT I had decided to make my home for my simple year is at the northern end of a range of domestic offices that make up one side of the yard. The larger section of the building, at the southern end, was a barn when we first came here. We did the minimum of restoration and alteration and have used it as a gallery for occasional exhibitions. The whole range has lost its slate roof, which blew off some time during the 1970s. It was replaced with red concrete tiles. They are ugly, but moss flourishes on them, so that the roof has a shaggy, green overlay, which looks like decaying thatch. There were many times during the winter when I wished that it really was thatch: it would have been so much warmer. When houses were given slate roofs, they may have become more watertight, but the loss of insulation must have made them miserably cold.

The walls are mortared whinstone, lime-harled on the outside. On the barn door, pencilled names of the children of James Nicol, the minister from 1802, show that the building stood here from the earliest years of the nineteenth century. Even some of the plastered walls in the barn have pencilled initials on them. The few bits of plasterwork in the cottage, however, don't. The walls there are mostly unadorned whinstone, with the new partition being boarded in local larch. This does not look too much like those traditional, V-boarded interiors that are familiar from Highland croft houses. Those all date from the fairly late nineteenth century. We were trying to create the impression of an earlier interior, with irregular-sized boards. When they weathered, I knew that they would look more at home in this vernacular room than any factory-produced material.

So, when it came to the new board floor, I resisted any impulse to seal it with varnish and oil. The fresh, new floorboards soon became grey and somewhat stained, like the school floors of my early childhood. I still fretted that I was wrong in assuming that a dominie's house would have been given such a luxury as early as the 1790s, for, at that date, dominies were very badly off. Their salaries, which varied from parish to parish, had been decided during the 1690s, when most of the village schools had been set up. They had not risen at all after that, although the cost

18

My mossy roof.

Old graffiti on the inside of the barn door.

My cottage looks strikingly similar to the one opposite, top: the engraving is by Thomas Bewick, who documented eighteenth-century scenes in meticulous detail.

of living had gone up considerably, especially at the end of the eighteenth century. By the time that the First Statistical Accounts were being compiled in around 1790, there was much grumbling on the part of the dominies: "To one who must dress, and is supposed to live, a little above the common lot, it is only a genteel kind of starving... But we shall cease to wonder when it is observed that, although the wages of the very lowest employees have doubled, and in many instances tripled, those of the schoolmaster have not altered for a century." (First Statistical Account, Borthwick, East Lothian.)

The houses provided by the heritors were described by various dominies as 'mere hovels' and frequently consisted of just a single room. There were complaints from the dominies that they could not afford plastered walls or coved ceilings. When, a little later (in 1803), The Schoolmasters' Act decreed that, in each parish, the heritors should build a two-roomed dwelling for their dominie, there was more grumbling, this time from the heritors. "Are we to build palaces for our dominies?" they demanded in more than one parish. One minister's suggestion was even more extreme: he thought that his parish should not improve the houses at all, but should instead get on with enclosures. If a field had good hedges and ditches, he argued, then the dominie, when he wanted to prepare a lesson (or even the minister, when he was working on a sermon), could go and sit in the 'hedge bottom'. 'There they don't hear, nor are disturbed, nor are diverted by the children's crying, or the Mistris and the Servants speaking loud about their domestick affairs, from which noise there is no room in the house remote enough.' [Mackintosh, William, *An Essay on the means for Inclosing (sic), Fallowing and Planting, etc, Scotland.* Edinburgh, 1792]. One can only assume that he was writing during the summer and was cursed with a very limited imagination!

All of these fragments of information add up to a picture of the utter simplicity of the dominies' dwellings. Apart from the wooden floor (and surely there is a longing for refinements in the complaint about lack of plaster and coving), it seemed to me that the cottage that I was putting into living order was very much the sort of place that a schoolmaster might have lived in. In reality, it probably started life as a manse, and may then have become a service cottage for the newer, grander manse that was built here from 1791 to 1792.

It was November 2004 when Jim, who usually comes once a year to do some pointing on the garden wall, arrived to sort out the chimney and replace the rotten window frames. John Behm, an artist friend whom I had asked to do the woodwork, appeared right at the end of the month. He brought some splendid oak-panelled doors for the box bed; they resembled a picture of panelling from a box bed in Orkney, and would do handsomely. He had rescued them from a bonfire. We were both amazed that anyone could even think of burning such solid and well-made things.

John also brought the wood for the partition that we were intending to construct. Its purpose was to shelter me from the fearful draughts coming in under the original outer door. I did not want to change the historic fabric of the cottage in any way, yet nor did I want to suffer from its inadequacy. For this reason I was ambivalent

My 1860s range is an anachronism, but it seemed to me a reasonable compromise.

The panelled doors of my box bed separate my sleeping quarters from the space I occupied through the day.

about completing the break-up of the single-roomed cottage into one with a small entrance room and a larger, 'L'-shaped space. There are precedents for this. Moirlanich Longhouse, near Killin (which is in the care of the National Trust for Scotland), for instance, has a baffled entrance in which you go into a passage before gaining access to the main chamber. As for local examples of the right date, I had none: there are precious few humble buildings that survive in the Borders. In the end, I just had to accept that it was not possible, on my small budget, to make everything completely authentic. We would have to do what was most practical, using appropriate materials, and would have to recognize that there would be some compromises.

The biggest compromise was the range. My ancestor, Anne Houston, would probably have cooked on a raised hearth, unless her cottage was wholly unimproved, in which case it would have been on a hearth at floor level. I had designs on a raised hearth with a hanging lum, which is a hood that hangs over a fire to conduct the smoke into a primitive chimney. I looked at the remaining hanging lums and discovered that they were nearly all constructed out of wood, sometimes with an overlay of papier-mache. It's hard to think of dafter materials to use for a chimney! No wonder house fires were relatively commonplace. I talked to a blacksmith about building a hood out of metal, but we couldn't see how we could make it work well enough to direct all of the smoke into the chimney, which was in the centre of the rubble wall.

Instead, John arrived one day with an old range. He had picked it up years before from an Edinburgh street. It dated from about 1860 and had been manufactured by Smith & Wellstood of Falkirk. Although it had been originally designed for burning coal, there were now such critical parts missing that I would only be able to burn wood in its tiny grate. Yet that fitted in well with both the grates and the fuel that would have been around during the 1790s. And the range would be simple to install, with a stovepipe heading through the wall more or less in the same place as the pipe from a much earlier stove. Here was a solution to what had seemed an intractable problem.

We placed the stove on a big slate slab that had served as the bottom of a water tank up the hill. One short side of this tank was broken, but all of the other sections were brought down the hill, some on shoulders, and some on the local farmer's quad bike. Every one of them found a use. One side became a windowsill in my 'real' house; another was pressed into service in the little entrance room that we had created in the cottage. Placed on top of an old workbench, I saw it as an ideal surface for the water bucket and washtub, and for washing up. Even the short end had a use: a maker-friend, Martin Murphy, trimmed it, bevelled it, and gave it an inscription. It then found its way to a Norfolk churchyard to become a memorial for my parents.

Building work went on until Christmas, with family, friends, and anyone else who happened to turn up being pressed into service to nail up the larch lining boards. My younger son, Ben, and his girlfriend, Caroline Brimmer, worked hard at it. Electric drills whizzed and saws ripped through planks – it was all very unhistorical because we were running out of time. The *Herald* reporter was due to come with a photographer just four days after Christmas. He was to write a feature to introduce my monthly column and the place had to be finished before they inspected it.

A table and three chairs completed my furnishings for the cottage. I sat here to eat, sew, write and – occasionally – just relax!

I used period drawings like this as sources to design my clothes.

My summer outfit is practical and comfortable.

I had all of my clothes for the simple year to finish, too, for it seemed important to dress for my decade. Research into appropriate costumes had occupied me, on and off, for months. Most of the period costumes that survive are grand dresses. And while there are paintings and drawings of aristocrats and working people, there are very few of members of the professional ranks, particularly in a rural context. What would a dominie's wife have worn? Edinburgh women were already making use of 'mantua makers' to sew fashionable dresses whose designs originated in London and Paris, but, given her financial constraints, my woman must have had something much more homespun. She would surely have made her own clothes, as most women did at the time. Mentions in contemporary accounts of sums for 'gowns' refer to dress-lengths of material, not to finished garments.

I read as many sources as I could, and looked at the work of the Scottish artist, David Allan (1744–96), who was painting at around the right time, and at the prints of John Kay (1742–1826), the Edinburgh caricaturist. Eventually, I came up with a day dress that was based on Kay's pictures of Newhaven fishwives, whose eighteenth-century costumes became fossilised as traditional wear and survived in hardly modified form until the twentieth century. From them, I took the full folds of my two (sometimes three) petticoats, my striped aprons, and my 'shor goun' (short gown), which were all essential for keeping me warm in the winter. I could not lay my hands on hand-woven wool, so I chose a grey herring-bone tweed as the next best thing. This made the outer shell. An old blanket, dyed dark blue, made the under-petticoats, which were visible, at least in part, because of the habit that people had of 'kilting up' their top petticoat.

HOW TO MAKE A SARK

The basic sark, or shift, is comprised of rectangles. The main piece of fabric is twice as long as the desired length of garment, plus the length of the sleeves, including an allowance for hems and seams. Traditionally the sark was worn at mid-calf length. Cut the fabric to a suitable width, if necessary, before you begin.

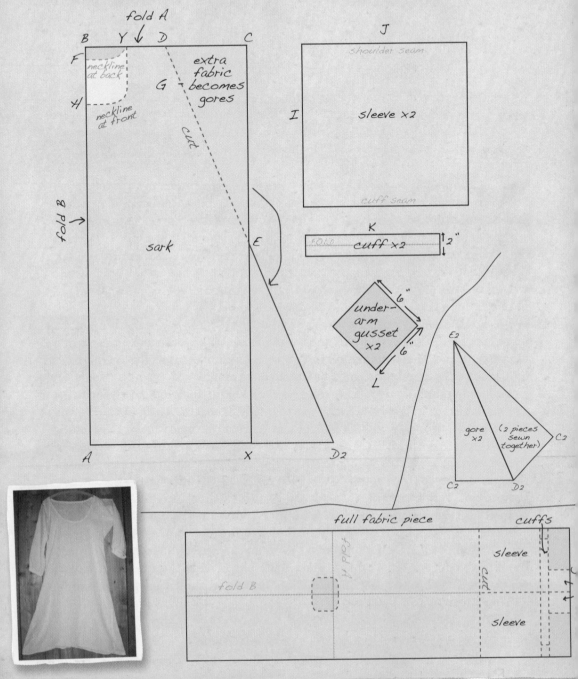

fold A

B Y D C

F neckline at back

extra fabric becomes gores

G

H neckline at front

cut

fold B

sark

E

A X D2

J

shoulder seam

sleeve x2

I

cuff seam

K

FOLD cuff x2 2"

under-arm gusset x2

6"

6"

L

E2

gore x2

(2 pieces sewn together) C2

C2 D2

full fabric piece

cuffs

fold A

fold B

cuff

sleeve

sleeve

1. Cut the sleeve pieces from one end of the fabric, ensuring that the sleeve length (edge I) includes an allowance for the shoulder and cuff seams. Decide on cuff width and depth and cut accordingly: the fabric will be folded in half to create the cuff, so if your depth is 2", your cuff will be 1" deep. Cut 2 underarm gussets (approximately 6" square) from fabric scraps.

2. Fold the remaining length in half across the width for main garment.

3. Fold again in half, along the double length, creating four layers of fabric.

4. Measure halfway along UNFOLDED (C-X) edge and halfway along top FOLDED edge (B-C). Mark. Check that the shoulder width (twice the measurement of B-D) will fit comfortably across your shoulders. Cut E-D through all the layers. Cut each offcut piece in half along the folds D-C to create four triangular pieces. Stitch one pair of gore pieces together along D2-E2, and then the other pair, to create two kite-shaped gores.

5. Measure B-Y and B-H on front surface of folds. Draw in curved front neckline as shown on top surface of folded cloth.

6. Reverse folding of A-B and draw in line Y-F (back of neckline).

7. Unfold as necessary to cut front and back necklines along lines you have created. Make paper templates to duplicate the exact curves for the second side of each neckline.

8. Attach E2-C2 edges of gores to each side of lower half of garment, E-X.

9. Stitch sleeves along length (I) to form tubes, leaving about 2" at one end for the cuff opening and 5" at the other to accommodate the gusset. Gather sleeves along their cuff ends, matching length of gathered ends to desired cuff length.

10. Form cuff by folding along strip K and seaming each end. Reverse the cuff and gathered sleeve and stitch sleeve into cuff.

11. Stitch two sides of the gusset into the open sleeve seam before presenting sleeve to garment. The prepared sleeve should look like the diagram at right.

12. Pin sleeves at D-G on each side of sark, starting at the centre of the shoulder and sleeve folds. Point G on the sark should correspond to a point approximately halfway down the sleeve's open edge. Pin point L of gusset to point E of sark.

13. Once you are confident that the positioning is correct, seam sleeve shoulder and remaining gusset edges to sark on each side.

14. Finish neck with tape, ribbon or bias binding. This must be done by hand! Then hem the garment.

Originally intended to preserve the top layer in a clean state so that it could be hastily let down when important company appeared, kilting seems to have become a fashion. It makes the hip-line very bulky. I was definitely going to have to get used to having a very full appearance, and to lacing myself into a bodice each morning. I decided on a soft bodice, rather than stays. The latter were certainly worn by more wealthy women but they cost so much that I guessed that a dominie's stipend would not have stretched to such a purchase. I still don't know whether that surmise is correct, but it suited me as I could make a bodice with ease. Stays, on the other hand, would have taken me weeks to construct, even if I had used a sewing machine.

In addition to these garments, I had my shifts, or 'sarks', to make. Two I cut from old linen sheets, making two others from new lawn, as cottons were definitely coming into Scotland during the late eighteenth century. The pattern that I used (see previous pages) was a time-honoured one for shirts and undergarments that dates back many hundreds of years. All of the sections are rectangles, although the main one, which is folded along the shoulder-line, has long, triangular pieces cut from it down, towards the waist. This process shapes the top and at the same time yields two panels, which can be let into the lower half to expand the hemline and make the garment less tube-like. The arms are indeed tubes, but are made workable by the addition of under-arm gussets. Almost no fabric is wasted. For my headgear, I chose muslin. Fashions seem to have shifted during the 1790s, from a true 'mutch', which was like a lightweight bonnet tied beneath the chin, to a more English-looking mob-cap. I made both. The mutch proved most irksome to wear, so I soon settled for the more English style, sometimes decorating it with a band of coloured ribbon, as can be seen in some of the

Here I am dressed for winter, complete with my cloak.

I found my lightweight mob-cap surprisingly comfortable and practical.

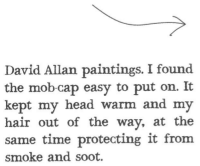

The cottage illuminated with soft light, looking like a Vermeer painting.

David Allan paintings. I found the mob-cap easy to put on. It kept my head warm and my hair out of the way, at the same time protecting it from smoke and soot.

By 29 December we were presentable. The photographer arrived and went into ecstasies about the contents of the cottage and the quality of the light inside it. "It's like walking into a Vermeer painting", he said. The reporter joined him, interviewed me in the cottage, and then repaired with me to the warmer surroundings of the main house's kitchen. I have lived here for so long that I forget how an old-fashioned kitchen, stone-flagged, with a dresser and a farmhouse table rather than modern units, appears to others. He was taken aback. "If you will forgive me for saying so, you're not making that great a change in lifestyle", he commented. There was a little truth in that, although daily life in the cottage was, in fact, tougher than anything I ever experienced in the house. Even during the winter of 1996, when the water was frozen for three weeks and there was no electricity for several days, the kitchen was never as cool as the 41–43°F (5–6 °C) that was the cottage norm during the winter months.

The final days of the old year disappeared in finishing off carpentry and preparing a party. My two sons and their partners were inviting lots of friends: I was allowed a few, too. Mine joined me for supper, so a dozen crowded around the kitchen table, whilst most of the young people cooked themselves a meal in a neighbour's house. We had cleared the drawing room for dancing so that I could go out in style. I joined in the reels, my tartan silk-taffeta skirt (a charity-shop bargain!) twirling. My dancing grew wilder as the apprehension mounted: before midnight, I would have to take myself away. The situation reminded me of a nun's initiation, although it felt more frivolous.

My visitors' book with quill pen.

At ten to twelve, I donned my many-layered garments, put on my mutch and my shawl, and came down, unnoticed by the crowd, to watch our customary New Year rockets. I beat all the company to the cottage and was there to greet people. My first job was to strike a spark with my tinderbox, light a 'spunk' and get a candle burning. I had been taught the process by a kind man, Patrick Cave-Browne, who knows more about making fire than anybody in Scotland. Although I'd practised it, I was apprehensive about getting the method to work, but it did. With my burning candle, I lit my carefully laid fire and was able to invite everyone into the cottage. They crammed in to sign the visitors' book with a quill pen dipped in homemade ink. A young woman I didn't know was exclaiming, "What shall I tell them in London? This is the most amazing New Year I have ever spent!"

As the young people went back to the dancing, neighbours appeared to wish me well. A dozen crowded in. The chairs were all taken, so Gerald, my nearest neighbour, perched on the end of the range. He had failed to notice the candle that I had burning there, and, seconds later, a flame shot up his back. I had to scuttle across to put him out. His coat was a write-off, and his jumper singed, but fortunately he was unharmed. How cautionary for me to have such a near miss within minutes of starting my simple year! I resolved to be vigilant with candles, and with sparks from the fire. Conflagrations may have been commonplace in the past, but I could do without that particular piece of authenticity.

My tinderbox, which I soon learned to use effectively.

Good old-fashioned revelry, fit to see in the New Year!

CHAPTER 3
The Business of Living

D AWN CAME SLOWLY that New Year's Day in 2005. I had no idea what time it was when I could see well enough to dress, mend the fire, take out the slops, and bring in more wood. In the yard I encountered Jane Brimmer, a house-guest, who had got up to walk her dog. Ghillie, my old black labrador, and I joined her for a twenty-minute stomp up the hill. I had left the porridge on the range, but when we got back, I found that the fire had subsided and that the oatmeal had scarcely cooked. The little brass skillet that I was using had to be nestled down into the embers, where its contents soon began to simmer.

I was serving the porridge in wooden bowls when Jane's husband, Martin, appeared. There was just about enough for him, and a scraping for the dog. Feeling that we needed more to eat, I half-filled the skillet with milk, added a good knob of butter and some salt and put it back on the fire. I didn't realise it at the time, but this marked the start of what became a daily ritual of making the dough for barley bannocks.

The whole process proved difficult that first morning. The girdle had been off the fire and had cooled down. I had to stoke up, blow on the embers to get a blaze, get the girdle into position and then roll out the bannocks. Because I had no rolling board, barleymeal showered everywhere. I dropped the thick stick that I was trying to use as a rolling pin and found myself apologising. Jane and Martin sat and grinned. A few years of cooking on a solid-fuel-fired Rayburn in their remote farmhouse in the Lake District had taught them patience; they live without mains electricity, and with only occasional use of a generator. So waiting for meals was nothing new for them.

To amuse them while we watched the girdle, I started to tell them what Dorothy and William Wordsworth had had to say about barley bannocks. They had travelled to Scotland in September 1803, staying in inns or cottages, depending on what was available. 'Oaten and barley bread', which means bannocks (what Robert Burns called 'cakes' in his description of Scotland as the 'land o' cakes'), was offered to them almost everywhere they went. Wheat bread, and the ovens in which to cook it, were almost unknown in the Scottish countryside at that time, as only larger towns had bakeries. The Wordsworths frequently found the oatcakes too hard but Dorothy conceded that barley bannocks, 'if they are thin and eaten hot', were good. I aimed to make them just like that.

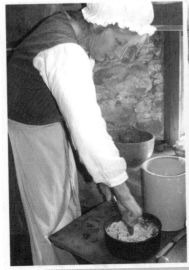

Making bannocks soon became part of my daily routine, once I had tended to the fire in my range.

I had a long wait to see light in my 'bedroom' that first day.

I can't think that I succeeded on that first day. But my guests were enthusiastic, and the bannocks had a taste all of their own. Later, when had I mastered the art of cooking them, I was able to present uniformly cooked cakes, crisp on the outside and a little soft within. They could be likened to chapattis and had a 'bite' that was very satisfactory. One visitor remarked that he was so gratified by eating them that they must be as good at releasing endorphins as chocolate is reputed to be. The idea is remote from eighteenth-century Scottish thinking, but he was right: barley bannocks are addictive!

All the while the kettle, which stood next to the chimney of the range, was near enough to the fire to get warm, but not to boil. It had to be put among the embers to speed it up to make some tea. I had filled the big black vessel to the brim, so it was taking hours. We began to try to work out how I could improve its performance. I already had a smaller, copper kettle, which would have done the job better, but it was leaking. If I could get that one mended, I could use it for the actual boiling by filling it from the warm reservoir of the big kettle. If only there were a tinker to hand! We talked of our childhood memories of these itinerant craftsmen who mended our mothers' pots and pans, and wondered how many other people could still recall them.

Breakfast over, it occurred to me that I had not yet washed. There was still some hot water left for some minimal washing up, but not enough for washing me as well. I opted for the breakfast things and then crossed the yard to fill the kettle for the next round. But so many people dropped by that day that I don't think that I ever did wash. I was on my way to acquiring an authentic patina before I had even got through the first twenty-four hours.

PORRIDGE! The Once and Future Scottish Food

If you have not already done so, forget ready-made breakfast cereals and go back to porridge. According to my Uncle Jack, it has to be eaten standing up, with your back to the fire. Scottish folklorist Marian McNeill tells us that in the Highlands, porridge was always thought of as being plural, so that you ate 'them' standing up. I can't say that I did so in the cottage, however, except when it was especially cold, and I certainly do not these days.

You can make porridge with ordinary porridge oats in five minutes, and with jumbo oats (which make good porridge) in a few more. But the real stuff is made with oatmeal. This has a higher vitamin and mineral content than rolled oats, which are processed with steam, causing some of these valuable elements to leach out.

There are many ways of cooking porridge. If you have an all-night heat source, such as an Aga or a Rayburn, it can be made simply by adding water to the oatmeal in a pan, covering it, and putting it in the coolest oven overnight. Failing that, it can be cooked the night before: put it on, as your grandmother might have done, when you are clearing up after supper. The cooking time is approximately twelve minutes, plus a brief reheating time in the morning.

1 to 1½ oz oatmeal per person, depending on how thick you like it
½ pt water per person
a little salt, added just before the porridge is eaten

You can either just mix the ingredients together in a saucepan the night before and then put it on a moderate heat (note that although you could use a microwave, you would sacrifice the nutritionally valuable forms of Vitamin B in oats by doing so) or you can follow the traditional Scottish way of making porridge. To do this, put the water in the pan, bring it to the boil and then add the oatmeal in a continuous stream, stirring all the time until the mixture comes back to a simmer. (The advantage of this approach, although it is slightly trickier, is the interesting texture and taste that you get. Each grain is discernible, and the flavour is a touch more nutty.) Carry on stirring from time to time to stop lumps from forming. Let it simmer for about ten minutes (a bit more if you are using pinhead oatmeal) and then set it aside. It will reheat in a very short time in the morning, and as long as you don't put it on too high a heat, you won't have trouble cleaning the pan.

Serve with one of these toppings, or else invent your own: yoghurt, grated apple, prunes, raisins, honey, brown sugar or milk.

Breakfast of champions! Oatmeal provides excellent nutrition and is warming on a winter's morning. →

Brose

An almost forgotten alternative to porridge is brose. It's quick to make and has a much stronger and nuttier flavour. You probably need to use just a little more oatmeal than you do for porridge in order to have a satisfying helping. Brose can also be made with peasemeal, which is known as 'brosemeal' in Caithness and Sutherland. It was traditionally a breakfast food, but its strong flavour may be a bit taxing for modern tastes.

2 oz medium oatmeal (or approx ½ oz per serving)
salt to taste
knob of butter (optional)
2 fl oz boiling water, or a little less for a thicker consistency

Simply put the oatmeal in a bowl with the salt and butter (omit the latter if you don't want it) and pour over boiling water, stirring (with the shaft of a horn spoon, according to the old recipes) until you have a 'knotty' mixture. (If you stir it too much, you'll get a thin paste; the knots form just before you get to this stage.) Eat your brose quickly, as it cools down rapidly. For the same reason, it's best to use a heated bowl.

Thus started the pattern of the months to come. I constantly crossed that yard for water, for kindling and to deal with ashes, going in a different direction for wood, and in another to get to the garden. When I was forced inside the house to my office to work on my writing or museum research, I went to and fro across the yard all day long, clocking up miles a day. I am sure that the past was characterised by this level of activity. Our ancestors were not sedentary but were constantly on the move, frequently having to bring water from much greater distances than my tap in the yard, and certainly having to range far afield to find fuel.

My own wood supply was already partly in place. Much of it was provided by fallen branches from my own patch, although I had bought in a load of logs the year before. We have always managed to operate a good wood rotation system: the wood is split and stacked in a well-ventilated log shed, to be used only after the lapse of at least one year, and preferably two. This is a luxurious set-up. During the eighteenth century, the majority of the rural population were living in such simple houses that storing wood must have presented a considerable problem. The local architecture cannot have helped. In many countries, the houses have overhanging eaves, beneath which wood can be stacked. That was not the case here, however, and wood or peat stacks had to be made separately and covered as well as possible. A peat stack can be built with an angled top, which sheds water well, but it is much more difficult to protect wood from the rain unless a freestanding roof is built over it.

And that is supposing that there was wood to be had, for the combination of the poor state of Scottish woods and the system of land-ownership made it a rare commodity in many parishes. People were reduced to burning whins (both gorse and broom can be referred to by this name) or, like many rural people in poorer countries even today, to drying cowpats for fuel.

My axe, which I found myself wielding with surprising gusto, and my split logs seasoning in the log shed.

A batch of bannocks rolled out and ready to go.

Bannocks cooking on the hot girdle, below.

BARLEY BANNOCKS

Barley bannocks are almost certainly the most ancient form of bread consumed in Scotland. Before cast-iron girdles were made, they would have been cooked on a stone.

The bere, or bear, specified in this recipe is a primitive form of barley that is now grown principally on Orkney. The bere bannocks that are commonly on sale there today are a later version that is made by including wheat flour and a raising agent.

Barley bannocks are best eaten straight from the girdle, when they are crisp on the outside and slightly moist within.

For one batch:
½ pt milk
less than 1 oz butter
salt to taste
5 oz bere or barley meal

Heat the milk, butter and salt in a small pan until the butter melts. Remove from the heat. Stir in the bere or barley meal until you have a sticky dough that comes away from the side of the pan (a bit like choux pastry). Turn on to a floured board and pat into a round. You can roll this out to less than ½ inch thick and cook it on a moderately hot, ungreased girdle or heavy frying pan for a few minutes on each side. I prefer to cut the dough into small pieces and form them into thick patties. I then roll these out fairly thinly, to a size a bit larger than a digestive biscuit. They will cook in about ten minutes (five minutes for each side). The dough patties can be stored for a day or two before being cooked. This batch yields 8 small bannocks.

MASHLUM BANNOCKS

I tried making mashlum bannocks and found them nourishing, but probably a bit outlandish for modern tastes. To make them yourself, mix barley, oatmeal and peasemeal with wheat and rye flour in any combination of quantities you like and then cook the mixture as outlined in the recipe for barley bannocks (page 35). You could also vary the ingredients. I have thought of incorporating seeds, such as sunflower and pumpkin seeds, which were not available to me in the cottage. It's always worth experimenting.

Much as I enjoyed chopping the wood, carrying it back to the cottage was a chore I disliked. A full cran is surprisingly heavy and unwieldy, especially in icy conditions. Baskets in the outer room of the cottage (top left).

A Bewick engraving of someone carrying wood. →

Little to do in the garden this month but dig or pick vegetables as needed. Keep an eye on apples and onions in store to sort out any bad ones. Time for house improvements like making drying rack, or draught-proofing windows and doors, during precious daylight hours.

Collecting and preparing wood became a major part of my morning chores. I dragged home branches from my early walk with the dog, and hacked at them, or jumped on them, to reduce them to burnable lengths. I learnt to split logs with a felling axe. This is traditionally a male role, and one that my sons compete for. I soon saw why: it's fun! Once you have discovered the technique of sliding your hands up the shaft of the axe, you can raise it with minimal effort and let it fall with a satisfactory 'clunk' that sends billets flying. The activity raises a sweat, bearing out the old saying about wood warming you more than once. The more difficult part for me was carrying a full basket inside. I was using a cran, the old fishing basket from which an imperial measure was derived. You used to be able to find them washed up on the shores of Skye. Traditional crans have long been replaced by plastic versions, but I still had a couple of ancient ones. A full cran is as much as I can comfortably carry, and when I look at pictures of women with creels on their backs, I see that their baskets are not much smaller – our foremothers were strong women.

I, too, was toughening up, and my days began to fall into a rhythm. As soon as the light outside was strong enough, I prised myself out of bed. Donning a shawl and some handmade felt slippers, I would then look to the fire. I could usually revive it with some small twigs and a good deal of blowing. Just occasionally, however, the hearth was really dead and I had to start again, using a tinderbox. Flint struck on steel over scorched linen produces a glow; this can be translated into a flame with the use of a spunk, which is a spill dipped in molten sulphur and then dried. Once a candle is burning, a fire can easily be kindled.

As soon as my fire was established, and the kettle was on, I allowed myself to cheat. My usual morning habit has always been to go up the hill with the dog before breakfast. I know that lots of people kept dogs in the 1790s because some of the ministers gripe about it in the First Statistical Accounts: 'They speak of themselves as poor but they

37

can afford to keep dogs'. However, I doubted whether hard-working people would have dreamt of just going for a walk. Dog-walking therefore being a luxury and an anachronism, I decided to go (unwashed) in my jeans, wellies and waterproofs. My cheating would also save my woollen clothing from an extra drenching and would allow time for the kettle to boil.

Half an hour later, I would, on good mornings, return to a steaming kettle. I usually made herbal tea: from lemon balm and from some peppermint dried from my summer harvest, from rosemary, or, like the old man whom Dorothy Wordsworth discovered collecting this plant in the Clyde Valley for 'his winter tay', from wild marjoram. I soon took to making the porridge in the kail pot the night before so that it would stay warming whilst I poured water into a broad, terracotta and cream-glazed pancheon for my strip-wash. I had to be brave for this because even indoors, it was still cold enough to see your breath.

I imagine that, for most eighteenth-century people, it was more trouble than it was worth to have a thorough wash each day. But my twenty-first-century habits died hard. Besides, the Georgian upper classes clearly thought washing necessary. In her *Memoirs of a Highland Lady*, Elizabeth Grant recalls the childhood horror of being plunged into an icy trough in the yard – the maids obeyed their orders, but would weep in sympathy for their charges, clearly thinking the procedure barbaric. Yet the habit of cleanliness stayed with Elizabeth. She later complains of a governess who refused to allow the young people to wash in the morning, but expected them to leap out of bed, wipe their face and hands and then dress, all in the space of ten minutes.

❀   It used to take me longer than that to complete my toilette and get into my elaborate clothes: the linen sark, the bodice, the two thick, woollen petticoats, my good apron, followed by a coarse apron, and over it all my short gown. After all of that, I was more than ready for my porridge.

By mid-January, my initial novelty value in the neighbourhood had worn thin. I was now well used to walking about in my petticoats, and most of my neighbours were, if amused by it, tolerant of my doing so. I felt a little sorry for the odd drivers who spotted me in the dusk as I crossed the road – they must have wondered what they were seeing.

One afternoon I was sitting near the window of the cottage, using the very last of the daylight to finish some sewing, when I heard men's voices in the yard. Curious, I slipped out and stood in the doorway. Two burly Scotsmen were trying to get water from a defunct tap at the churchyard end of my building. I recognised the local slaters, the men who repair my roof each year. The sound of my latch made them look up, whereupon they froze and their ruddy faces suddenly drained to white as they stared at the apparition in the doorway. They thought that they were seeing a ghost! It was only when I spoke that they moved towards me and saw who I was. Explanations followed. Both were quite tickled by what I was doing. Writing for a newspaper seemed a good enough excuse to be wearing fancy dress. They went away, chuckling.

Despite the cold and the long hours of darkness, winter has a beauty all its own: moody skies, and frost edging the leaves and trees.

That incident helped to prime me to venture further afield. I had coasted through early January on Christmas and New Year leftovers. Some kind friend had brought me milk and I had needed nothing else. Now I wanted butter, cheese and more milk, but I somehow felt timid about walking the 3 miles down the road to the village to get them. My friend Mary, visiting from the south, gave me the confidence to do so. Here is that day's diary entry:

Walked to Innerleithen with Mary. A dreich sort of day but we were merry enough on the road. We saw a Kingfisher from the bridge over the Tweed. It was flying along the wooded channel that runs parallel with the main river. Almost a first for me in twenty years of living here, although I think I once saw one near the Traquair House pond.

Adrian Keddie, the butcher, and his wife made a point of coming out of the shop to greet me and offer me their fine, old-fashioned bacon. But in the Post Office, where the people are new, they made no comment about my fancy dress. We carried out our transaction as though nothing were odd about my standing there in antique dress, in a cloak, and with a ridiculous mobcap on my head.

I wonder how long we will keep that up.

When we reached home, I found that my cloak was saturated from the hem upwards for about a foot, and that my petticoats were pretty wet, too. That was from walking on tarmac. How can it have been on the muddy tracks of the past?

My larder in January:

From store: potatoes, carrots, onions, dried peas, dried beans, apples

From garden: parsnips, leeks, swedes, kail, winter cabbage, sprouts (these were not in seed-lists but I had grown them and was not going to let them go to waste because they were historically inaccurate!)

Cabbage

Sprouts

Leeks

My other diary entries for January record the arrival of visitor after visitor. I was not going short of company, although I was starting to find the evenings a trial. I could only read for a short time by candlelight and I was sorely missing my usual companion, the radio. The reality of having no music on tap for a whole year seemed an appalling prospect. There were wonderful moments, like the one when I stepped out of the cottage in full moonlight and saw the shadows of the trees dancing on the stable wall and my own moon-cast shadow sliding across the yard. But my state of mind tended to be gloomy during the long evenings.

To cheer myself up, I planned a party for Burns Night (25 January) and invited the neighbours. There were eleven of us in all, including a girl from China who was visiting one of my friends. I walked to the butcher's again

A damp, chill January day.

Traditional Burns Night fare: haggis and neeps.

41

Thomas Bewick's engraving of an eighteenth-century feaster who appears to have over-indulged!

An old-time winter ceilidh.

to buy three haggis and spent hours chopping up my best neeps from the garden and peeling quantities of tatties. With only one large pot, I had to plan the cooking carefully. I steamed the potatoes in a cloth above the neeps, but the pot took hours to come to the boil. I was stoking the fire all afternoon. With so much fuel being heaped on to it, the whole range got hotter than usual. The cottage became warmer and even the oven, which normally acted as no more than a storage space, heated up enough to keep the vegetables warm whilst the haggis went into the pot to cook in their turn.

The neighbours arrived in different levels of fancy dress. Brian and Pam had hired theatrical costumes and looked like lairds. Others sported car-rug kilts or tartan shawls, which were needed, for although the cottage seemed tropically hot to me with all of those people in it, most of them still found it chilly. Everyone had been asked to bring something to read or recite, and Gerald's offering, harking back to my first night, was inspired:

'Gerald, Gerald, burning bright
In the byre, where day is night.'

CHAPTER 4
Daylight and Dark

ONE OF MY REASONS for trying to go back in time was my anger at our throw-away society. It's not just the wastefulness of buying goods, using them for a short time and then chucking them out that upsets me. It is the whole swathe of human activity and endeavour that is negated by this cycle. In the past, people had fewer resources. They had to use their skills and ingenuity to obtain the things that they needed for daily life. They had to make, mend, improvise and invent. I like all that. I may not have all of the skills, but I have the inclination. In deciding to live simply for a year, I was setting myself a challenge to let the practical side of my nature come to the fore.

During my 'year in the past', doing things was not just a physical but a psychological necessity. It was not difficult to keep active during the daytime: I had my basic chores to do, as well as walks and attending to visitors; I had letters to write, seams to sew and vegetables to prepare. I quickly learnt to use every moment of daylight. But the evenings were becoming an increasing torment. Sewing by candlelight is just as taxing as reading beside a flickering flame. What I needed was some other form of handwork that I could do in poor light.

And now Ben and Caroline came to my rescue. They had visited Dove Cottage, in the Lake District, where the Wordsworths had lived for some years, and were struck by the rag rugs that formed the only floor covering. Back at Caroline's parents' remote house, they set about finding a sack on which to work and plenty of old clothes to cut into strips. Jane Brimmer kindly lent them two spikes for pushing the rags through the sack to make a traditional 'proddy rug'. This, they brought to me when they had done a few inches of the dark, outer rows, which were a feature of the original rugs that they had seen.

My rag rug, with the two hand-made spikes.

←

This is the outer room of my cottage, where I washed my dishes (and myself!) The dish-drying rack I improvised, seen to the right at the back of the surface, was pleasingly effective.

The rug project was a boon. I loved using the handmade spikes. One was made of roe deer antler, polished by use to a glassy finish. The other was a whittled-down dolly peg, of at least World War II vintage, and possibly much older. Having two tools, I could let friends join in with the work. It was gratifying, too, to be frugal in using up rags to make something that would be useful.

The second new skill that I decided to acquire was that of broom-making. When Mary came, the two of us went out to gather birch twigs. We chuckled about the appropriateness of two crones setting about making besoms (brooms made of twigs tied onto a long handle). The process looked simple enough. We chose strong hazel sticks for the handles and bound bundles of thin birch twigs tightly to them. They weren't very even, however, and it was difficult to stop the bundle from spinning on the stick. What we should have done was to make the bundle separately and then hammer the stick through it, but we only got round to reading how it should have been done the evening after we had completed them. At least they worked.

It was not long before I had to put my ingenuity and practical skills to the test again. For the first weeks in the cottage, I had washed up my supper things, standing in semi-darkness in the narrow, cobbled outer area and stacking them to dry on the slate-topped workbench. It was January. The temperature was low and the humidity, high. I piled things onto the slate to drain. Each item made a dull 'clunk', causing me to fear for the two hand-thrown bowls and the couple of (almost) period teacups. Everything would then sit there in a pool of water. This was no good for the wooden plates and bowls, or for the horn beakers that made up the rest of my tableware. Nothing ever dried. Necessity now stirred up invention, as I had hoped that it would.

Dim memories of bushcraft skills, square-lashing and knotting, came back to me. I went off to the orchard and cut some straight hazel poles from a bush that we had coppiced two or three years before. I chopped these down to convenient lengths and set about making a drying rack. I ran out of daylight as I worked, and had to sit on the cottage floor, a candle beside me, labouring away to finish it. Then I ran out of short sticks for the main drying surface and grew low on twine. Impatient to finish it, I lit a candle in a little tin lantern and went off to the woodshed to see if any of the kindling sticks would do. More string came to hand in there, too, attached to old beanpoles I had stored away for the winter. Now I was able to get on with the square-lashing. I also remembered to put in some diagonal bracing, the result being that my drying rack turned out to be stable enough to satisfy even a sceptical son. Having made it without help from anybody, particularly 'blokes who know best', I was ridiculously proud of it.

And my drying rack worked well, too: plates stood up in it and both of my little wooden brushes had their niches. Even my ancient knives and forks could rest there, needing no more than a quick rub with a cloth to stop them from going rusty. These implements were of old-fashioned carbon steel, the forks three-pronged, the knives wickedly sharp. I had bought them from a junk stall when I was fifteen. I acquired my teacups a little later, along with a Georgian tea caddy. The copper kettle was a twenty-first birthday present. It was as though I had been preparing for my time lapse for most of my life.

Not everything that I used was old, however. The wooden bucket in which I carried water, for instance, is a lovely piece of modern cooperage from Finzean, in Aberdeenshire. I went there to write an article about the recently restored nineteenth-century mills, and succumbed to buying this proper Jack-and-Jill pail. It pleased me then simply as a handmade object. It proved invaluable for cottage life:

There are moments when I am handling my pail, walking across the yard with it, or lifting it to pour the last water into a pitcher, when I really do seem to catch the past. I feel like the woman pouring from a jug in the Vermeer painting. I know it's the wrong century, but my costume, with its short gown, is so like the blue garment worn by a woman in another of his pictures, that I feel myself to be right there.

Treasured and well-used items: my wooden pail and the kail pot.

I found myself wishing that I could afford a second wooden pail. But instead of spending another £70, which would have been nearly three weeks of my living allowance, I had to invent the notion of approximation. I would have had a strong aversion to the suggestion of hiding a plastic bucket under the slate bench. Instead, I found a white enamel one, which was about eighty years old, judging from its style. It was made in a factory, which was a compromise as I preferred everything to be handmade. But as there was no drainage, I had to have a slop bucket. (A household with only one bucket must have been truly poor.)

Most of what I had collected over the years cost very little. My bargains – the kail pot, the Scotch frying pan, the girdle, the big black cauldron in which I cooked all the food on Burns Night – are all bits of Scotland's past. The problem is that there are too few people who value such things. I used to be indignant about this, but just a couple of months of living in a simple cottage taught me to be more forgiving. Life in the cottage, the fermtoun and the sheiling was a grind. And for many, that era continued well into the twentieth century. No wonder people reared in the smoke of an open fire, without running water or drainage, snatched at progress. No wonder that there is, even now, little respect for the material remains of the past. That past is too humble, and too recent. This indifference is sad enough when it applies to tools and tackle, like the unfortunate collection belonging to the former folk museum in Glenesk, Angus, which is now without a display space. It is even sadder when it applies to buildings. A friend of mine, who is an inspector for Historic Scotland, reports that he is frequently accosted by people intent on getting rid of old houses. He may be looking at a neat little eighteenth-century cottage like mine, but along they come, swearing that it's a disgrace and should be pulled down. The poetry of Burns may be honoured, but the houses of his contemporaries are, in many places, still being demolished.

As February wore on, I rejoiced not only in the return of migrant birds, but in the return of daylight in the early evening. Suddenly it was possible to manage simple indoor tasks like chopping vegetables as late as five o'clock without resorting to lighting a candle. But the end of the month brought a different problem: snow.

The snow caught me when I really had given up expecting it. But then there came a wickedly cold night when, even though I was huddled before the fire, my hands were blue. I shut both shutters, stuffed some fleece into the skylight and sipped a hot toddy before going to bed with my hot stone. My diary for that day reads:

My clogs are no good in deep snow.

Snow complicates things. I can no longer trot in and out in my Galloway clogs. I have to wear my Oxfam leather boots, thankful that I've got them. Few women, even respectable ones, wore shoes. Dorothy Wordsworth, visiting Dumfriesshire in 1803, remarks, 'met two well-dressed travellers, the woman barefoot'. John Ballantyne, who is in his seventies, can even remember women with bare feet and red legs in Glasgow shops in the late 1920s. My quest for authenticity stops short at this point. I shudder at the thought of crossing a snowy yard in bare feet.

February 12th. Warm day: metallic green flies on snowdrops in the churchyard. I have always wondered why these winter flowers had a scent, and here is the answer.
Leaves are coming on honeysuckles in the hedges and on the elder by the compost heap.

February 14th. Owls hooting all night. They must be breeding.

February 22nd.
Oystercatchers calling last night.

February 27th. Daytime barn owl sighted over melting snow. Wonderful camouflage.

But falling snow did awaken enough of the child in me to entice me out for a second walk. It took me through conifers that had grown so thick that the snowflakes could not penetrate them, except where the path was wide. It was like being in a series of rooms, each walled with laden branches. In front of me, there were shafts of light, full of snow, like giant motes of dust. It was lovely, but I was conscious, all the same, that this was an alien sight for Scotland. During the 1790s, sitka spruce was unknown here. Apart from the odd yew tree at the top of some Highland glens, the only large evergreen conifers were Scots pines. Several of these lined the end of the path. 'Splendid trees', I thought, but it was one of them that rewarded me with snow down the back of my neck. Then a vista of birch trees, their fine branches feathered in white, opened up. It was a sight that must have pleased people, time out of mind.

My larder in February

From store: potatoes, onions, carrots, dried peas, dried beans, apples

From garden: parsnips, leeks, neeps, kail, winter cabbage

Cabbage

Neeps

FEBRUARY'S CHORES

- Dig first broad bean trench and sow
- Sow brassicas in trays indoors

Chopping firewood remained a daily task throughout February — and well beyond!

←

OATCAKES

I found it difficult to turn out good oatcakes when cooking on my girdle. I tried many recipes, including the one given here. My best results were obtained when I used the whey from cheese-making instead of hot water. Baking in an oven, while not traditional, is easier, yet I still find myself buying, rather than making, oatcakes.

Marian McNeill's Oatcakes

4 oz oatmeal
1 pinch baking soda (or bicarbonate of soda)
1 pinch salt
1 tsp melted duck, chicken or goose fat, or of butter

Put the dry ingredients into a bowl. Make a well in the centre, add fat, and then add hot water (or whey), a little at a time, to make a stiff dough. Knead rapidly, and then turn on to a board that you have dusted well with oatmeal. Roll out to ⅛ inch, cut into quarters (farles) and cook, smooth side uppermost, on a moderately hot girdle until the edges begin to curl. Remove and finish cooking by toasting the smooth side in front of a bright, smokeless, fire. Alternatively, place on a baking tray and cook for about twenty minutes in a moderate oven.

Marian gave me the valuable instruction that I should store the cooled oatcakes in the meal kist; if you bury them completely, it keeps them fresh. This quantity yields enough to make eight farles.

Gathering wood for burning was another regular chore.

51

I am eating well. It's porridge and barley bannocks in the morning. Broth and bannocks or oatcakes usually make my lunch, with a little of the cheese that kind friends seem to bring with them when they visit. In the evening, I have vegetables cooked in various ways. Stovie potatoes are great. I make them in a heavy pot, with half an inch of water and a little duck fat. I just scrub the potatoes, slice them and pop them in the pot. On a good fire, if I stir them from time to time, they will cook in half an hour. Yesterday, on a slow one, they took all afternoon. Neeps and parsnips, with a few coriander seeds and perhaps some bacon, respond very well to the same treatment. They make a dish in their own right.

Trees laden with
new-fallen snow.

Tramping home, I realised that my boots might serve for gardening, but that they had given me a blister. I shook out my cloak, assessed the dampness of my petticoat hems (they were soaking) and stoked up the fire, ready to cook.

I would stir-fry leeks or cabbage in my Scotch frying pan, adding whatever took my fancy from my store of dried herbs and my spices. It was often caraway seeds that went in, something that could have come straight from by the front door of many a Highland croft house. Stir-frying may sound a modern approach, but the technique of cooking with a little fat, and then a little water to steam the vegetables, is traditional. Some recipes for the wonderfully named rumbledethumps, a mixture of cabbage and potato, suggest precisely this way of cooking the cabbage.

STOVIE POTATOES

Don't be shy of using the animal fat suggested here. There is a strong argument that we have got it wrong about the merits of vegetable fats, apart from olive oil, and that the demonising of animal fats may be ill-founded. A little duck fat used for frying once in a while is delicious, and much better for you than margarine or many vegetable oils. This is a good way of using up old, overwintered potatoes.

  good-sized knob duck fat (or slug of olive oil)
  ½ lb potatoes per person, peeled and cut into fairly thin slices
  a little water
  salt and pepper
  dried mixed herbs to taste

Grease the base of a thick-bottomed pan with the fat or oil. Add the sliced potatoes and water, dust with the seasonings, put on a well-fitting lid and place over a very low heat. Shake from time to time. After fifteen minutes, check and add a little more water and/or fat if necessary. The length of time that the potatoes will take to cook will vary according to the heat, but will probably be about an hour.

RUMBLEDETHUMPS

This wonderfully named dish from the Borders reappeared during World War II as 'champ'. Use these quantities for four people.

  2 lb potatoes
  1 lb cabbage or another green vegetable
  butter or margarine
  1 cup milk
  salt and pepper

Cook and mash the potatoes. Chop the cabbage or greens finely and then cook in very little water with some butter or margarine. Combine the potatoes and cabbage or greens, adding the warm milk. Add a knob more butter, plus salt and pepper to taste.

Stoved Root Vegetables

- coriander seeds
- duck fat, butter or olive oil
- neeps
- parsnips
- carrots
- celeriac (optional)
- herbs, such as thyme or marjoram, to taste
- a little water, salt and pepper

Allow about 4 oz of vegetables per person, plus a
little 'for the pot'. Grind the coriander seeds coarsely in a mortar
and pestle. Melt the fat, butter or oil in a heavy pan that has a lid.
Stir in the crushed coriander seeds and then add the vegetables,
cut into thick slices, and any herbs. Stir well to distribute the fat,
butter or oil. Add enough water just to cover the bottom of the
pan. Reduce the heat to a whisper, clamp the lid on and cook for
about forty minutes, checking at least once to avert the danger
of sticking. Season once the vegetables are soft to avoid making
the dish too salty.

My other spices were whole dried root ginger, cinnamon bark, whole nutmegs, pepper and blade mace. All were available during the eighteenth century. They lived in a pretty wooden box, from which I got such pleasure that I found myself showing it off, along with the special mortar in which I did all of my grinding. This is a broken half of a prehistoric stone bowl. (My childhood mentor was an archaeologist, and I inherited many wonderful items from him.) The bowl is probably Mediterranean, but early Scots made them, too. If you visit the Crannog Centre in Perthshire, you can try your hand at the technique that they used for boring into stone.

The hens had started to lay well, so on one night a week I was eating eggs. On another, I had some of the peas that I had dried the year before. They, and haricot

New-laid eggs.

54

The prehistoric bowl I used as a mortar is among my most treasured possessions.

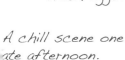

The hens provided me with a steady supply of fresh eggs.

A chill scene one late afternoon.

beans (also from the home-grown store), had to be soaked overnight and then cooked slowly for a long time. On some days, the range kept at the right temperature. On others, I had to be patient and feed the fire in order to finish them off. Served with some onions and bacon, they made a good dish. About once a week, usually when I was entertaining, I cooked meat. Sometimes this had been given to me by visitors. One brought two big chops of wild boar, another, a joint of goat. Beyond these, I ate road-killed rabbits or pheasants, collected locally (a modern phenomenon, but a good replacement for having a regular hunter around all of the time), or, on a couple of special occasions, I culled one of my own poultry. Whatever I had, it went into the kail pot, sometimes to stew alone or else with onions. Or

I would make hotchpotch. This dish, a thick stew containing meat, carrots, peas and turnips, was served by Lochiel, the renowned Jacobite, to his guests at Achnacarry in 1734. No one in the Highlands had seen these vegetables before, and the surprised local gentry were soon ordering the planting of kitchen gardens so that they too could cultivate them.

So during those cold evenings I would make up the fire, pull my shawl around me and sit at my little round table, working on my rag rug, which kept my knees warm. I was content. The room had a kind of beauty, especially in candlelight. I enjoyed its plenishings: the pewter mugs, the big-bellied storage jars ('pigs', as they were called) and the cran that served as a log basket. Like all of the objects that surrounded me, they are part of history – my own, and that of people who had lived before me. I reflected on how they all had stories to tell.

Hotchpotch

3 lb neck of lamb (or another cut)
3 handfuls pearl barley
choose several from: carrots,
     turnips, onions, cauliflower,
     celery, broad beans, peas, shredded
     lettuce or any other vegetables
a handful of parsley, chopped
salt, pepper and mace (a very
     eighteenth-century spice) to taste

Put the meat and barley in a
saucepan with about 3½ pints water.

Bring to the boil and skim off any scum that forms. Simmer for two hours, then add any root vegetables (chop them first) and celery (if you are using it). Cook for a further hour or so. Twenty minutes before serving, add the cauliflower, broad beans, peas and lettuce (if you are using them). Before you serve the hotchpotch, remove the bone from the lamb's neck and snip the meat into small pieces with a pair of scissors. Return the meat to the pan and add the parsley. Adjust the seasoning if necessary and then serve with bread or barley bannocks (recipe on page 35). This makes a feast for six to eight.

৶ CHAPTER 5 ৶
Am I Doing This Right?

HAVING ESTABLISHED MYSELF as an eighteenth-century matron, I found that I had a problem when circumstances obliged me to step back, or rather forward, into present time. The moment came when I knew that I would have to throw off my period clothes for a day or two and bring myself back in line with present sensibilities. I gave myself one of my weekly 'cottage baths'. For this I boiled up both my big kettle and my large pot. Standing in front of the fire, I reluctantly (because it was cold) stripped off and then made myself squat awkwardly in the wooden washtub. This was made of planks – not staves, like the pail – and was of approximately the right date. I certainly found an illustration of an identical one dating from the early nineteenth century. It was fine for washing clothes in, but was too small to sit in for a personal scrub-down. There was enough hot water in the tub for me to have a total wash. I found that it was useful to have rinsing water (at a reasonable temperature) standing by in the pail, with a pitcher to hand so that I could sluice the soap from every bit of me.

I dried myself with a linen towel dating from 1830, part of a wonderful pile of linen that I had bought from an antique-dealer friend. Every towel and sheet is dated and initialled by someone from a different generation of the same Highland family. There is even one bearing the numbers '96' in cross-stitch. I have no proof, but it looks to me as though that means 1796.

Once back in a clean sark and clad in petticoats, I considered my hair. I had avoided washing it, and it was starting to change. My diary records what happened next:

People have told me that within six weeks, hair will settle into a natural, healthy, glossy state. I've been hopeful that this would happen. Perhaps in clean surroundings it would work but mine just feels stiff and lacklustre. I suddenly felt an overwhelming need to wash it. I had to heat up yet more water and clean out the washing-up crock. I couldn't see where to put it: it was too cold in the outer room, and I didn't want to slosh water on the round table. In the end, I put a stool on top of the kist and set the bowl on that. Before I launched into the process, I filled up a second basin with warm water for rinsing. What a palaver! I decided to use just a tiny bit of the good olive-oil soap that I was given. Dirt poured out! All the smoke and ash particles of five weeks!

It took me an inordinately long time to heat water and prepare everything I needed for bathing. Washing pots – or oneself – outdoors must have been miserable except in high summer.

The following morning, I dressed in normal clothes and walked down to catch the bus (the 'honorary stagecoach', as I said to myself) to Edinburgh. Despite my changed attire, I sat in that bus puzzling over the problem of transport. If I wanted to be historically accurate, I was probably failing by being on the road at all. The first part of the journey was allowable as the turnpike road from Innerleithen to Peebles was built during the 1790s. Carriers may have plied between the two places, but as for a coach service to Edinburgh, that had only been available a couple of times a week. It would have taken all day for the vehicle to make its way from Peebles into the city because the carriage road had not yet been built. That did not happen until the first decade of the nineteenth century. This late development of road-building was common to most parts of Scotland, making it very unlikely that a person like my ancestor, Anne, the dominie's wife, would have contemplated such a journey.

The reason for all of this preparation and sacrifice of authenticity was persuasive enough, though: my first grandchild had just been born! I was off to meet him and to congratulate my son, Ram, and daughter-in-law, Charlotte. I was so excited and keen to get to town that it surprised me that I was feeling ill at ease at having stepped out of my eighteenth-century role. Walking about Edinburgh, I felt conspicuous. I worried in case I met someone who would challenge my right to be there and question my modern clothes. It didn't happen on that occasion, although I had to face up to exactly that sort of scrutiny later in the year. The elation that I felt once I had my first cuddle with the new baby, Ruairidh, put paid to all of the soul-searching. I went off to celebrate the new arrival with a friend and then came home again by bus the next day without a flicker of self-consciousness.

The general problem of authenticity went on bothering me, though. The iron range was the compromise that I was regretting. It gave the cottage such a nineteenth-century appearance. When David Jones, from the University of St Andrews, wrote to say that he was coming, I was nervous. David is a vernacular-furniture expert and probably knows more about humble Scottish interiors than anyone. Would he dismiss my attempts to recreate the 1790s as fanciful, or just too fancy?

Maybe David was just being generous, or maybe he really did like the cottage. He enthused about the round pedestal table and the three simple, baluster-back chairs (they look right because they are right). He liked the pewter candlesticks, even though they were early-twentieth-century fake antiques, and the tallow candles in them. I only had a few of these, which were donated by my fire mentor, although I was planning to get on with making lots for myself (see Chapter 12). Having an expert visit, this was not the day to be caught out with the gross anachronism of the paraffin-wax candles that I had been obliged to use up to that point.

David also admired the box bed, although he commented on how unusually wide it was. The width had been dictated by the size of the former workbench around which it was built. The old 'Scotch double', whether a box or a free-standing bed, typically measured 4 feet x 5 feet, 6 inches. My recess was both wider and longer, although the size of my mattress wasn't.

The mattress was the cause of great grief at around that time. I had stitched the ticking bag before Christmas and had stuffed it with wool left over from the insulation that we had inserted into the partition wall. Once I got used to its firmness, it was quite comfortable. For the first few days,

I learned at great cost that the mattress HAD to be turned regularly.

It was fascinating to hear an expert opinion on the authenticity (or otherwise) of my furniture.

I assiduously turned it each morning, and that kept it sweet. As time went on, I grew lazy. Weeks had passed before one breezy day I thought, 'I'll turn the mattress and change the sheets', forgetting that I had lapsed in performing this housewifely duty since early January. But there was something nasty in the box bed! As I heaved it over, I was aghast to see . . . mould! The bottom of the mattress, which had been lying directly on the boards of the old bench, was damp and disgusting. I suddenly understood an old aunt's lifelong preoccupation with airing things. My feeling of guilt at failing as a guid-wife was heartfelt.

Out came the wool stuffing. I sponged down the bag and pegged it on the line. Part of the sheet was mould-speckled, too. It was one from my big batch of linen, and was of the old Scots style, 13 or 14 feet long. In eighteenth-century Scotland, if sheets were used at all, beds were universally made with just one long one. This covered the mattress, was folded at the bottom, and then ran back up the bed to serve as a top sheet.

'I'll wash that sheet now!' I thought. It was a fine day, so I set up my washtub on its stand outside. The kettle was full of hot water intended for washing up, so all seemed easy. A good scrub shifted most, if not all, of the nastiness. I toiled to and fro across the yard carrying rinsing water, and then, with difficulty, wrung out and hung the huge sheet on the line. With a good breeze blowing, I had the satisfaction of hearing the washing whip-cracking away, knowing that it was drying well.

Before dusk, I went out to fetch the sheet in. There, a new horror greeted me: the clothes prop had blown down. All day, the sheet had been flapping on a molehill. A corner was filthy, and a brown stain was radiating outwards, into the sheet. What was I to do? I swore a little, but didn't have any qualms: I bundled the sheet into the basket, stormed down to the house and shoved it in the washing machine. Edinburgh trip aside, it was my first major cheat!

My bedding.

Heather makes a comfortable (and traditional) mattress stuffing.

Fortunately, the ticking bag had more or less dried. That now came into the cottage to air for a few hours. Much later, I found myself in the stable, stuffing straw into the ticking bag to make a palliasse by the light of my candle lantern. Now, there was authenticity! Well, maybe. Straw was indeed once used as bedding, most often in loose form as a literal 'shake-down' bed, or for some male travellers who were not admitted to the house, but had to make do with the byre or the stable. And the most frequently used mattress-stuffing in the fermtouns was chaff. I had read about this, and had thought how lumpy and dusty such beds must have been. I didn't expect to meet anyone who had slept in one. But much later in the year, my neighbour brought her mother to visit me. The old lady had been brought up on a farm in Dumfriesshire well before World War II. As a child, she had had a 'calf-bed', as they called it, which was, in fact, a chaff one. Yes, it had been dusty and lumpy. It also was a haven for mice. Despite all of this, there was a fond thread of nostalgia running through her recollections.

Straw proved an adequate alternative to wool. That first night, when the palliasse was thick and well stuffed, it seemed heavenly. It was soft and warm, so it didn't matter to me when it crackled as I rolled over. After a week of use, it had humped up in some places and pitted in others. I had to shake it out regularly, and I still had to make sure that my whole bed was aired every single day. The technique that I used was to strip back the sheet and woollen blankets each morning, and then to drag the cumbersome palliasse back into a giant fold, in one direction one day and in a different one the next. An hour or two later, I would have to come back and make the whole thing up again. Compare that with the careless shake of a duvet!

As the straw lost its bounce relatively quickly, with each piece flattening under my weight, I later looked in vain for an alternative stuffing. Heather was suggested. Although this was a traditional bedding material, the design and height of my bed made it impossible to use heather in a traditional way. The very best beds were made when bundles of well-grown heather were cut and forced into the bed frame, with the growing tips uppermost. More and more were crammed in until the whole frame was densely filled. A blanket was then placed over the top and the sleeper simply lay down on that, as though he or she were stretching out on a moor. It was said to be extremely comfortable, and to last many months, so I wanted to try sleeping on a heather bed. Alas, I was only ever to simulate it with clumps of heather on the hill, where a good growth can really cradle you.

With the extra time that I was obliged to devote to bed-making, carrying out ash, sweeping, fetching wood and water and washing small items, the mornings were taken up with chores. The burden of the chores, and the ambivalence that I felt about wearing my costume, are repeated themes in my diary entries.

After a day or two of restlessness and resentment about the stupid clothes and the time that it takes me to get things done, today I was at peace with it. I had a lovely hour this afternoon, reading Marjorie Plant's book about domestic life in eighteenth-century Scotland and drinking a cup of real tea, something that I usually reserve for visitors.

Sometimes friends would arrive early and catch me out:

Susie arrived when I was still in my jeans, washing up with the scullery door ajar to let in light. I heard the car and scuttled off to change, appearing without my cap to greet her. It didn't matter that I still had the fire to do and the floor to sweep as she was here to sketch me, and relished anything that looked different and interesting. She remarked on the very strange shape that my clothes give me.

On other occasions, I acquitted myself rather better:

A good day: I have done it all by the book and in good time. Fortunate, because John and Bron showed up before 10. Instead of slumming it in my jeans, I was clean and dressed and cooking the vegetables for my broth. I made a big pot, using the remains of the weekend's pheasant stew as a basis.

Cooking was a major occupation. Because of my frequent visitors, I felt that I always had to have a good pot of broth to offer. There were still plenty of leeks in the garden; kail, too, was abundant. In store, there were potatoes, carrots and onions. And I occasionally remembered a hidden resource like Jerusalem artichokes – delicious, but dire in their effects on the digestive system!

Would an eighteenth-century schoolmaster's family have had so many visitors? I pondered on that, not that I could (or wanted to) stop people from coming. I resolved the question in my own mind by regarding my visitors as substitutes for a sizeable family. And having to feed more than just myself made the experiment more realistic. At the end of the year, when I studied my diaries and added up all of the meals that I had cooked, the number of meals that I had shared turned out to be equal to having at least one other mouth to feed, day in and day out (see pages 210–13. When I came to read John Galt's *Annals of the Parish*, I formed a picture of the social life of the 'better' inhabitants of a Lowland village. His account, although a fiction, is based on everyday life, and covers the period from about 1760 to 1812. It seems that there was a good deal of socialising, with women calling on one another to drink tea in the afternoons, and men visiting each other of an evening to discuss politics, as well as the new Enlightenment thinking that was spreading from its Edinburgh stronghold into even rural Ayrshire, where Galt's fictional parish was situated.

A late eighteenth-century raised hearth looked much like this, sometimes with a smoke hood called a 'hanging lum'.

MY FOOD IN MARCH

From store: potatoes, carrots, onions, dried peas, dried beans, apples.

From the garden: parsnips, leeks, swedes, kail, spinach (all shown in the photos).

'MEAGRE' BROTH

You can use this broth as a vegetable stock to provide a basis for other soups or eat it, either clear or thickened, as a light spring or summer soup.

Simmer all of the ingredients in a pot of boiling water for about an hour. Strain before serving (you can give the soggy vegetables to the chickens or put on the compost). Served with bannocks and cheese, this makes a good light lunch.

To make 2 pints stock/soup:

Two handfuls of spinach
2 or 3 outer stalks of celery, with leaves
3 or 4 green onions
2 small lettuces (outer leaves or ones that are starting to bolt will do)
several sprigs of parsley
good-sized bunch mixed herbs
salt and pepper

My Chores in March

- Dig first pea trench and sow
- Make onion beds
- Plant seedling brassicas out in rows in cold frame when they are large enough to handle.
- Direct sow kale where it is to grow
- Buy seed potatoes and onion sets
- Sow radish, lettuce and rocket under cover
- Sow leeks in seed rows under cover
- Sow parsnips in situ

Newly prepared raised beds for sowing or planting out.

NATURE NOTES

March 1st. Elm trees in flower near Traquair House. I've always liked the curious red bristly blooms they produce.

March 20th. Lots of birds singing now. I heard the first real curlew, though starlings have been imitating them for weeks.

March 22nd. The frogs are singing – great chorus from the pond for the last few days. I noticed the first spawn today.

CHAPTER 6
Friends Come Flocking

EASTER WAS EARLY in 2005 and the holidays brought still more people to see me. The first succession of them came from the south and stayed in the house, crossing the yard to breakfast with me. Most arrived in cars, but I persuaded them to abandon them at the front of the main house so that I would not have vehicles intruding on the yard, or visible from my living space.

I now became a little more self-conscious about making my morning trip to the privy. I had reinstated the minister's old earth closet, which is a small chamber at the end of the stable block. It faces the kirk, so it has always amused me to think of former ministers ruminating on the sermon for the week with their trousers down. Rather than use ashes, which were the favoured agent for such places, I decided that sawdust would work well in the bucket below the neat, wooden seat. A further box of sawdust and a scoop stood ready, as did a little pottery bowl in a small niche in the wall. I carried with me a small, lidded jug containing warm water, a clean rag and a towel. I will not go into details, but you can imagine that the procedure was effective, even if it took some getting used to. It was certainly better than using moss, although leaves were a useful addition when they were available. I could pluck lime leaves from a handy tree as I went in during the summer, although I found the system more difficult to manage in the heat because of flies.

Emptying the bucket was a weekly chore that I didn't much relish. I had set up a special composting bin with a lid, situated well away from everybody and everything. It worked. I knew that it would because I have a friend who lives in the woods near Ullapool who has used a similar system for years. As long as you don't allow the contents of the bucket to get too wet, the composting process starts quickly. That meant having to pee behind the bushes rather than resort to the privy. I also had to empty the overnight bucket on the normal compost heap, not into the dedicated bin. All of this was more complicated than the usual methods that the rural Scots once used for coping with bodily functions. In the winter, the women used the byre, which was usually attached to the house, and the men, the stable. In the summer, they either used a bucket or went outside, probably to dedicated areas. A luxuriant growth of nettles near, but not too near, the ruins of old cottages probably gives some indication of the whereabouts of such favoured places.

I never asked my visitors to avail themselves of these facilities, of course, and they never asked to do more than peep at them. Yet my reading revealed that when spinning and weaving were cottage industries, a 'pish barrel' was always kept near the dwelling. It was thought rude, in those days, if visitors did not contribute to it before they left. Following the advent of modern plumbing, we have grown too 'nice' to countenance this idea, but in the past, urine was a useful source of alkali for scouring wool and was used as a mordant for certain dyes.

My post-Easter guests were two whole families, one from Argyll and the other from Oxford. The house and garden rang with the shouts of mock sword battles, and walks were punctuated by burns paddled and trees climbed. All nine of the company (one was very small indeed) crowded into the cottage for one meal, but mostly they were self-sufficient. That was lucky because my own self-sufficiency was starting to become more precarious. I still had some winter stores – a few apples and plenty of potatoes, carrots and onions – but there were almost no greens left in the garden. I began to appreciate the critical importance of kail. This not only survives the winter, but when the new shoots start to grow in April, becomes sweeter and sweeter.

I am using kail to sweeten the broth. One recipe describes putting it in right at the end of cooking, which seems more sensible than boiling it for hours. Maybe the cook knew of James Lind and his discoveries about anti-scorbutics. When I read the First Statistical Accounts, it's plain that most ministers understood the need for fresh vegetables, but there are still a few who, even in the 1790s (sixty years after Lind?), were blaming scurvy on an excess of oatmeal, rather than an absence of greens.

Rosehips I'd collected previously, and then dried, were an excellent source of Vitamin C.

Scurvy was widespread during the 'hungry gap', that season when the old stores are giving out but there is nothing new to harvest. It nearly crept up on me. I found myself craving blackcurrants, and it did not take me long to ask myself why. One apple and a few potatoes a day would provide enough Vitamin C when the fruit and vegetables were fresh, but by the end of April, their vitamin content must have been flagging. My body was telling me that it needed more, just as had happened to my sister-in-law, who found herself buying parsley, three big bunches at a time. She would consume one on the way home from the shop and would then keep on chewing until the rest were gone. Weeks later, she discovered that she was seriously anaemic, and that parsley is a good source of iron!

I decided to listen to my body. At that point, like the sickeningly provident mother in the novel (and film) *The Swiss Family Robinson,* I remembered a little box of hedgerow berries that I had put aside in the autumn. It contained rosehips, elderberries and blaeberries, which I had dried out in the bottom oven of the Rayburn, thinking of them more as a treat than a medicine. In fact, they served as both. Rather than being severely sharp, like the commercial rosehip teas (which are mostly made of hibiscus, the cheap ingredient in nearly all of those fruit-flavoured teabags), the tea that I brewed was deliciously fruity. My sons may have teased me about being an old witch with her herbal brews, but that one did the trick: I stopped craving blackcurrants and was able to wait out the long weeks until strawberries came into season without feeling ill or utterly deprived.

I had other strategies for coping with the hungry gap, too. In common with the Highlanders of the past, I have always regarded nettles as allies. And as soon as there were a few inches of growth on the nettles in my patch, I was making soup with them. I have two methods for making nettle soup. Both involve frying the chopped nettles in a little butter, with a chopped onion (if you have one). When the leaves have softened, you add water and chopped potato, or else medium oatmeal, as a thickener. The soup then simmers for about twenty minutes. Seasoned with salt, pepper and a grating of nutmeg, it tastes delicious (see recipe opposite).

Nettle Soup

Highlanders once relied on nettles to flavour their broth during the hungry gap of April through June, when kail and cabbage were not available.

Remember to wear gloves when you cut, or pluck, a small basket's worth of young nettles, or, if they are older, nettle tips. Wash well.

An alternative is to omit the potatoes and to use medium oatmeal instead (about a tablespoon to each pint of water). Serves four to six.

2-3 medium-sized onions, roughly chopped
knob of butter
small basket young nettles, roughly chopped
2-3 medium-sized potatoes, roughly chopped
2-3 pt water
salt and pepper

Gently soften the chopped onions in the butter. When they are transparent, add the nettles and turn them for a few minutes until they, too, soften. Add the potatoes and water and bring to the boil. Simmer until the potatoes are cooked, then either mash up the mixture (if you are following the garden-cottage approach) or reach for the hand-held blender and blend. Season to taste.

SORREL SOUP

The recipe above can be adapted for sorrel soup by substituting three generous handfuls of sorrel for the basket of nettles. The tangy taste of sorrel is welcome after eating vegetables that have become bland from long storage over the winter. Sorrel also appears in eighteenth-century recipes, well buttered, as an accompaniment for flounders. (Alas, the Tweed at Innerleithen is so far from being tidal that flounders are not to be had!)

Another treasure of the wild is wild garlic (or ramsons). This grows in damp woods, and where it enjoys the right habitat, it flourishes. Near here, it has colonised a river bank woodland which is really the overgrown garden of a house that was demolished after World War II. By the end of April, it is coming up so thickly that you can pick baskets full of the leaves without making any impact on the vast clumps. You can eat it as a 'pot herb', meaning steamed or turned over in butter. The taste is oniony, and rather pleasant. It made a welcome change from spinach, which I was still picking about once a week. I have seen only a few mentions of Scots using ramsons as food, although mentions of medicinal applications for it abound in the folk records of the Highlands and Islands. The plant was used to break up kidney stones and cleanse the blood – what a shame that more people didn't eat it.

It was a house guest who suggested something more interesting to do with the wild garlic. He brought with him some olive oil, which appears in eighteenth-century cookery books, although it would have been unusual to have found it in any household but a wealthy one. However, I was feeling like a luxury and soon experimented with grinding raw garlic leaves and mixing them with olive oil and some lemon juice. It took a while to get the seasoning right, but the result was like a pesto (see opposite page). Not

WILD-GARLIC PASTE

Not all of the ingredients in this recipe are indigenous to Scotland, but this way of using ramsons is so good that I was prepared to use some of my small hoard of olive oil. This, the greatest luxury of my eighteenth-century kitchen, makes an occasional appearance in recipes of the period, although it would have been unknown in any humble household, as would garam masala. This paste is very good served with oatcakes (serves four to six).

2 large handfuls wild garlic leaves
2 oz hazelnuts
2 tbsp olive oil
1 tbsp lemon juice
a little sugar, salt and pepper to taste
a little garam masala to taste

In the cottage, I chopped wild garlic leaves and bashed hazelnuts, and then put the two ingredients into a mortar and thumped them into a paste with a pestle before adding the other ingredients. It's much easier to put everything into a food processor and then press the button.

wanting to use so recently imported a term, I called it 'wild-garlic paste' instead. But what could I serve it with? It was then that my friend came up with a splendid idea: he remembered the Derbyshire oatcakes of his childhood and went away to telephone his mother, who was able to recall the recipe (see overleaf). Derbyshire oatcakes are more like pancakes than their Scottish cousins. They are made with fine oatmeal and some wheat flour. The mixture has milk and yeast added and is allowed to rise until it is frothy. Once I got the temperature of the Scotch frying pan right for cooking them, I started to turn out lovely, honeycombed pancakes the size of the pan. These kept warm when stacked, wrapped in a cloth, and nestled near the chimney. When the stack was complete, I spread each one with the wild-garlic paste and rolled it up. They made a magnificent meal that cost virtually nothing but a little effort, and we speculated about what we might have been charged for them in a London restaurant.

DERBYSHIRE OATCAKES

This is a recipe from the mother of a friend. You can increase the proportion of oatmeal at the expense of wholemeal flour if you prefer. (And I frequently do.) This quantity makes about 16 oatcakes.

½ pt milk
½ pt quite hot water
1 tsp sugar
2 heaped tsp dried yeast
½ lb fine oatmeal (or whizz porridge oats in the food processor)
½ lb wholemeal flour
2 tsp salt
butter for frying

Combine the milk and water in a mixing bowl. (You are aiming for just above blood heat, so make an informed guess about how hot to make the water you use.) Add the sugar and yeast and then set the bowl in a warm place for about twenty minutes to get the fermentation process going. Now stir in the oatmeal and flour, adding the salt last. You should have a fairly thin batter. Leave this to froth up, which should take about twenty minutes in a warm place, but longer if it's cooler.

Now butter a frying pan and heat it well, but not enough to burn the butter. Use a cup or ladle to measure out a portion of the mixture into the pan, bearing in mind how many oatcakes you are aiming for. Fry the mixture over a moderate heat for several minutes, resisting any impulse to poke at it, or to attempt to turn it, until the top surface has dried and the edges come away from the pan. The second side will cook quickly. (I tend to have two pans on the go at the same time to speed things up.) Completed oatcakes can be kept hot by wrapping them in a cloth and stowing them in a cool oven, or they can be reheated later.

Rhubarb & Sweet Cicely

Choose the youngest, reddest stems of rhubarb that you can find. Cook gently with a handful of sweet cicely leaves and as little sugar as you can get away with. The herb seems to reduce the acidity of the rhubarb. Ginger and orange are also interesting flavours to blend with this early 'fruit'.

How dreich it has been. A pall of grey cloud has been obscuring the sky for days on end. Today, the sun finally came out and my spirits rose a bit. But I quickly got into trouble. I had been grubbing out spurge roots from the bed near the bird table, when I managed to run a garden fork into the back of my hand. It's a small puncture wound, but I am worried about it because now my hand is swollen and angry. I promised R and B that I wouldn't let my health suffer because of my historical experiment, so tomorrow I think that I will walk down to the surgery to get a tetanus booster and see what they have to say about it.

I did indeed take myself down to the surgery, where antibiotics were prescribed for my wound. But over the course of the second night, the swelling went on growing worse. By morning, I was stiff and in some pain. I thought that a poultice might help, so I looked at my old books on herbal medicine, which all suggested comfrey. The first comfrey leaves were just showing outside, so I gathered two handfuls and chopped them up. I then added a sprig of rosemary for its antiseptic properties, put everything into a bowl, and poured boiling water over the top. After a minute, I strained the leaves through muslin, wrung them out, and slapped the uncomfortably hot parcel on to the back of my hand. I bound on the poultice with more muslin and left it on for a couple of hours. When I took it off, the swelling that it had covered was dramatically reduced. The puncture, which had been closing over, was opening up and expelling nastiness. I repeated the operation with a larger poultice to cover more of my hand. By the time that the doctor saw it again, she was very satisfied: "Do it again!" she said. "It's just what that wound needed." I wished I had thought of the remedy earlier – perhaps I would not then have needed the antibiotics.

It took a week or so for my hand to heal properly. On Easter Day, I walked about 9 miles over the hills to lunch with friends who live in a restored peel tower. It was another dreich day, but the rain held off, that is, until I was on the hill road, within sight of the little castle, whereupon the skies opened. My host had seen the rain coming, too, and hopped into his

75

The buds began opening once the sun shone and the days were warmer and lighter.

car and scooped me up, wet woollen petticoats, shawls and all. I still hoped to walk home again later, but was overruled. In the past, I would have been forced to stay the night to wait for my clothes to dry out. As it was, hovering between the past and the present, I gave in and gratefully accepted his proffered lift home.

The sun finally shone on my birthday in the middle of the month. I was suddenly keen to shed my heavy winter gear and put on my cottons. But I had still not got around to finishing their hems and had to fall back on an old friend, a Laura Ashley pinafore dress, circa 1970, cowpat-green and bell-shaped, whose broad skirt has doubled up for many different periods in museum re-enactments. Covered by my long, stripy apron, and wearing my spencer (the style of short jacket that had become hugely fashionable by 1795) against the wind, my outfit proved just the job. The world was full of birdsong, and it felt a cheerful way to chime with the spring.

My hair, however, was not in tune with the day. It had been three-and-a-half months since I used a shampoo, and six weeks since my experiment with olive-oil soap. I hadn't repeated the latter because my head had itched for days afterwards. Instead, I had dunked my hair in warm water a couple of times. Now, stuffed inside my cap, my locks were feeling weary. Few historical sources mention hairwashing, although Dorothy Wordsworth's journals give a clue that it was actually done: 'Washed my head', she says, about every second month. I thought that I might try the same approach, still hoping that the natural oils would take over and give my hair some shine. Yet it continued to lack lustre.

NATURE NOTES

April 1st. Sunny! Ramsons are coming up. Had the first picking.

April 5th. Butterburs, with their curious beige-pink tufted spikes, are erupting on bank of Quair. The foliage follows much later and becomes as large as rhubarb leaves.

April 28th. 'My' swallow is back on its exact place on the gutter, twittering cheerfully. Is it really the same individual?

April 29th. Clear and cold. Caught the first scent of birches coming into leaf.

Then, as I was looking at Elizabeth Grant's *Memoirs of a Highland Lady,* I found an intriguing account of the Highland girls who 'had a custom in the spring of washing their beautiful hair with a decoction of young buds of the birch trees'. She went on: 'I do not know if it improved or hurt their hair, but it agreeably scented the kirk, which at other times was wont to be overpowered by the combined odours of snuff and peat-reek'.

I was keen to give it a try. With my skirt billowing, I set off with the dog and a leather satchel. Across the valley, I saw the birches, the rounded shapes of their canopies contrasting with the harsh outlines of the sitka spruce trees behind them. The birch twigs were still a handsome, brownish purple, although the first haze of green lay on some branches.

Collecting birch buds is a sticky business. They are tiny, and a handful accumulates painfully slowly. It doesn't offer the same rewards as gathering berries, when you can scoff as you pick, but I soon learnt to strip along a twig. All that I really missed was a companion. I'm sure that the Highland girls would have gone out together, calling to each other and giggling as they planned their spring assault on the local lads. How they actually made their hair-wash, I didn't know. I would have to experiment.

I gradually settled into a rhythm and my mind wandered to the menu for my birthday party. The dog sloped off into the wood; she was rabbiting, which gave me an idea. But then she didn't catch anything, and rabbits are not to be bought in the village. If rabbits was what I was going to cook, I would have to walk 8 miles over the hills to the butcher's in town.

Home from the woods, I examined my spoils. Having had to look up 'decoction' (it means an extraction made by boiling), I swung the pot over the fire and watched as the water simmered and the buds turned yellow. The room filled with the fresh, peppery scent that wafts down from the woods on warm, damp evenings when the birches have really come into leaf. It's a marvellous smell, sweetly suggestive of summer. Yet the liquid was now turning green and starting to look like pond-slime.

Having no desire to transform myself into a Goth, I was nervous when I came to pour the decoction over my hair, in case it, too, turned green. But the results were pleasing: my hair really did smell wonderful, and if I fell short of the standards set by some advertisement woman, my locks suddenly did have a bit more bounce and shine.

My transformed hair helped me to feel good for my birthday feast, which I held the following weekend. I did make that trip to Peebles to buy rabbits. Another fine day saw me toiling uphill to join the high drove road that runs along the top of a fine ridge above the Tweed. The world was greening up. There was just a mist of green on the larches beside me, but the valley below showed a collage of colours, from the unnatural, dark shades of artificially fertilised fields to the surprising, yellow and bronze – and even purple – hues of trees' leaf buds waiting to burst. A round trip of 16 miles to buy rabbits might have seemed excessive on a bad day, but on this spring one, the walk was a pleasure.

Having one's hair washed
is not always a welcome
experience! →

Spring lambs and new
birch leaves.

Spinage (or chard) with Eggs

'Spinage', the old spelling of spinach, may seem comic, but crops up in most early recipe books. This is a simple dish that I cooked frequently, especially in the spring, when the hens were laying well and there were frequent rich pickings from the overwintered Swiss chard and perpetual spinach. If you grow nothing else, these crops are really useful stand-bys, and with good planning, fresh spinach can be available from the garden in almost any month of the year.

This dish is good with stovie potatoes (see page 53).

- one small onion, chopped
- butter
- two compressed handfuls spinach or chard per person, well chopped
- nutmeg
- salt and pepper
- cream (optional)
- two eggs per person

Soften the onion in butter, then add the spinach (or chard) and continue to fry and stir until it is well wilted. (New leaves cook very quickly, but overwintered ones will need a few minutes.) When the leaves are cooked, season with nutmeg, salt and pepper, add a little cream if you like and then break two eggs over the top. Put a lid on the pan and leave on a gentle heat for a further two or three minutes, until the eggs are poached (but don't let them become too hard). Sprinkle over a little more salt and pepper before serving.

My guests for the party were John Behm, my trusty house carpenter; his wife, Rachael Long; and their small son, Mungo; along with Ben and his friend, Richard. I found an eighteenth-century recipe, 'How to stew rabbets', and another for a pudding made with prunes and egg custard (see opposite). The food was absolutely authentic and turned out well. There was something discordant on the table, however: the boys had gone out of their way to purchase the most inappropriate present that they could think of: a McDonald's 'Happy Meal'. The sordid box sat there, its contents congealed. The toy was played with, but I decided that I could not bear to eat a burger, or even to have it second-hand, recycled into eggs after being fed to the hens. In the end, we gave it to the dog, who is not discriminating.

WHITE SCOTCH COLLOPS

This traditional collops (escalopes) recipe is given in my ancient cookery book for veal. It works well for young rabbits, too.

    two young rabbits
    a little flour, for dredging
    salt and pepper
    one egg, beaten
    about 2 oz breadcrumbs
    knob of butter
    four rashers smoked bacon
    a little sherry

Take the fillets out of the rabbits or get a butcher to do it for you. Use the rest of the animals to make stock, and prepare this before you want to cook the meal.

Sandwich the fillets between sheets of greaseproof paper and then beat them with a rolling pin to flatten and tenderise them. Dip each fillet in flour seasoned with salt and pepper, then in beaten egg, and finally in breadcrumbs. Gently fry the fillets in butter for five minutes, ensuring that they do not burn. Turn over each fillet, add four rashers of bacon to the pan and fry for a further five minutes. Check that the meat is cooked. Remove it from the pan and keep it warm. Add a little flour and a dash of sherry to the pan, then stir in some of the stock that you made earlier and simmer to make a sauce. Serves four.

STEWED 'RABBETS'

two young rabbits
a little flour for dredging
a little butter
stewing liquid: about 1 pt of broth or stock
  and 1 glass white wine
salt and pepper
bundle sweet herbs
mace
two small onions or shallots per person
several handfuls asparagus kail (or 'ragged Jack')

'Cut them [the rabbits] into quarters, dredge
them with flour, fry them with butter: put
them in a stew pan with some good broth, a
glass of white wine, and a little salt and pepper, a bundle of
sweet herbs tied in muslin with some blades of mace. Cover the
pan close and stew until tender.' From 'Receipts in Cookery', 1736.
When the rabbits are tender, peel and sauté whole in butter a
couple of small onions or shallots per person, and simmer the
rabbits a little longer. When the onions or shallots are nearly
soft, add several handfuls of asparagus kail and cook for a short
time, until it is tender (the new summer kail should be very sweet).
Combine and serve. Two rabbits will serve four.

A Prune Pudding

'Nine eggs well beat, a quart of cream or
new milk, six spoonfuls of flour, a little
salt and nutmeg; mix it by degrees into the
milk; add a pound of prunes and a quarter
of pound of sugar. Tie it in a cloth and
boil it two hours.' From 'Receipts in
Cookery', 1736. I adapted this by mixing the
dry ingredients, adding the milk/cream, and
then the eggs, gradually, stirring constantly,
then adding the prunes. I then boiled it in
a basin rather than cloth. The custard-like
pudding was good! Serves six.

MY CHORES IN APRIL

- Plant onion sets.
- Later in month, start potato planting, remembering that harsh frosts can strike in May!
- Prepare ground for summer vegetables and sow spinach.
- Make main-crop pea bed and second broad bean bed and sow.
- Make successive sowings of small rows of salad plants under cover.

- Collect dried oak-apples: the round, woody galls are easier to see before the trees come into leaf. Save for making ink (see page 110).

CHAPTER 7
Plugging the Hungry Gap

SPRING MAY BE GETTING going by May, but the problems that I had been starting to experience in April rapidly became more acute as the garden yielded less and less. The perpetual spinach (spelt 'spinage' in the contemporary seed lists) ran to seed and had to come out. The brassica tribe all ran to seed, too. I hacked back the small yellow flowers as much as I could to encourage new, broccoli-like shoots, but in the end I had to evict the plants as I needed the space for my carrot beds.

Even worse than that, the mice had found me! When I went to my store to get the very last of my apples, the little beasts had been at them. Wizened Ribston pippins that might have seen me through the month were inedible. I felt gloomy at the prospect of five months without apples, for it is at least September before any ripen in the orchard.

I did have just one more resource hidden away, however, and now was the time to find it. The year 2004 had been a good one for fruit, producing plenty of apples and plums. I had made apple rings and had experimented with drying plums. Being yellow, they made small, brown prunes, rather than plump, black ones, but they were nevertheless delicious. I rationed myself to one a day, with a small handful of apple rings, and hoped that friends might bring oranges. These were a treat that I had always been delighted to accept. Oranges and lemons had been available in days past in Scotland when ships came in from the Mediterranean or Africa, and there are records of them arriving in Thurso during the sixteenth century. They were clearly not everyday fare, but the accounts that I kept in the back of my diary reveal that I did allow myself to buy a lemon from time to time.

Mouse-traps and hungry cats – timeless solutions to the problem of mice invading the food stores.

84

I was very glad of my supply of dried apple rings and prunes once I ran out of my stored apples from the previous autumn. →

DRIED APPLE RINGS & PRUNES

If you have a glut of apples, preserving them without sugar, and without relying on freezing them, can be useful. Choose sound apples, and then wash or wipe, peel, core and slice them. I have a small machine for the purpose. It is a modern version of a Victorian invention, which is cranked by means of a handle to core, peel and slice all in one operation. It works well for regularly shaped fruit, but bumpy apples are too much for it. I then resort to a potato-peeler and a sharp knife – and bless the fact that I have them – as well as a metal corer. In the cottage, I had only carbon-steel knives, with fairly large blades, and a bone corer. (Some tools have improved with time and the introduction of new materials.)

To dry the apple rings, first dip them in a diluted salt solution for a moment to stop them from browning and to discourage the formation of superficial mould. Either spread them on baking trays and then dry them in the coolest oven or hang them on strings over a permanent heat source – (you could probably dry them in a warm airing cupboard). They will take from one to two days to dry, depending on how warm the place you choose is. Finally, store the dried apple rings in boxes or jars. They are delicious snacks to take on long walks with you.

In bumper plum years, I have prepared prunes in a similar way. You have to start drying these at a very cool temperature for twelve hours, and then raise it for another twelve or more. It helps to lay an old piece of cloth between the baking tray and prunes to stop the prunes from sticking to the metal. Turn them as necessary. In the coolest oven of my Rayburn, they take two days to become sufficiently wrinkled to store. These prunes are really good things to have to hand, either to add to cooking or just to munch when there is no fresh fruit around.

Supplies on my windowsill - including the 'exotic' lemon.

To deal with my need for greens, and to feed important visitors like Kitty Corrigan, the deputy editor of *Country Living,* who came to interview me for the magazine, I had to rely more and more on gathering provisions from the countryside. Wild saladings abound in the spring, and I tried all sorts of things. The best were the young shoots of Jack-by-the-hedge, hawthorn buds and the tiniest leaves of bishop's weed (ground elder). The latter have a delicious hint of aniseed at that stage, which grows too strong, for my taste, as they get older; then they are better steamed. When I combined the wild salad with a few leaves of rocket from an old plant in the cold frame that had started to shoot, I had something well worth eating.

Keen to impress Kitty, I went off to find more ramsons. I was down in the damp wood the evening she came, gathering a basket full of the leaves and flowers. As I clambered up towards the farmyard, I heard Ewan, the farmer, come out of his house and get on to his quad bike to go to check his sheep. Most people in the neighbourhood had seen me in my archaic garb, but Ewan hadn't, and I felt suddenly shy. I slipped the dog on a lead and turned back towards the river. It would be better to ford it rather than emerge from the trees and give him a fright. The dog and I were midstream, near the road bridge, when I heard the quad bike returning. We slipped in under the arch and stood, knee-deep in water (belly-deep in the case of the dog), whilst Ewan drove over the bridge, straight above our heads. The dog looked puzzled. Maybe the name 'ramson' gave me the cue, but I felt just like a character from an Arthur Ransome book: 'an Amazon', avoiding 'a Native'.

I had improved on the recipe for the spicy, green garlic paste (see page 73), so when Kitty was sitting wrapped in shawls in my cottage, I employed her. Issued with a couple of handfuls of leaves and flowers (which are equally good), as well as hazelnuts, she experienced what it is like to grind everything by hand using a pestle and mortar. A process that would have taken seconds in a food-processor demanded twenty minutes of vigorous activity. By the time we came to add the olive oil and lemon juice, Kitty had warmed up, the fire was burning brightly for my Derbyshire oatcakes, and we were ready to greet the *Country Living* photographer and his assistant with an exotic meal drawn exclusively from the Scottish countryside. Even the hazelnuts were home grown.

Kitty Corrigan was not my only media visitor during the spring. I had been in correspondence with Gabi Fisher, of the Radio 4 programme 'Open Country', for some weeks. Early one bright, but chilly, morning, she turned up with Richard Uridge, the presenter. Gabi is a one-woman production team. She does everything from research to recording and editing, and it was fascinating to work with her as she directed us to speak or to shut up so that she could record atmospheric noise, the fire burning or me sweeping away with the besom. At lunchtime, we were joined by some of my own team: John Behm and Patrick Cave-Browne, my fire mentor. John told of the process of making the box bed and the trials of working the green oak for the new doorframe. One post had had a curious shake in it, which made the saw stick; when he freed the blade, he discovered shreds of paper, the remains of some ancient notice that had been posted on the tree. Patrick enthralled everyone with his demonstration of how to use a tinderbox. He took us through the process, from the knapping of flint to make an edge sharp enough for striking the steel to the charring of linen for tinder. This was helpful because my supplies of sharp flints and linen charcoal were dwindling, and although Patrick had shown me what to do before, I had never found the time to do it.

Patrick's visit has replenished my tinderbox supplies. I've been assiduous in not using matches. Much of the time, I achieve that by keeping the fire going, but I have had to strike a light often enough to have become reasonably proficient. The 'spunks' P gave me are immensely helpful. Their sulphur tips catch readily when I rest them on the glowing linen charcoal and blow. I have to take care that the blue flames don't drip molten sulphur when I go to light a candle, but I usually succeed in getting a secure flame quite quickly. It must have been so much more difficult before spunks were invented. Then, people would have had to gather loads of fine tinder, dried grasses or tiny twigs to get a wee fire going in the tinderbox itself. Messy. And more time-consuming. I'm grateful for this 'intermediate technology', which is perfectly authentic. I've read of women hawking spunks, (ha'penny each, or three for a penny) on Edinburgh stairs in the late eighteenth century.

May is traditionally the month for 'getting the garden in' in the Lowlands. The herds and other labourers were hired for the summer at a fair at Whit, which was fixed as 15 May in the New Style calendar. When they went to their new hirings, their priority would have been to get a garden going. The timing also relates to the weather. We had night after night of ground frost that month, and if you have young seedlings emerging from early sowings, they can be scorched off by the frost, so it's better to wait.

Tatties and kail would have been the first things that went into the ground. I had finished my potato-planting by the end of the first week of May. My seedling cabbages, kail, broccoli and cauliflower were well up and pricked out into seedling rows in the cold frame, waiting for a cool, damp day in which to be planted out. The first peas and beans were up; those were sown in early March because they are hardy. I stuck brushwood around them to keep off the birds. I usually cover them with horticultural fleece, but I had to refrain from doing that for a year, for any casual visitor would see that that was not an authentic eighteenth-century method of gardening.

MY FOOD IN MAY

From store: potatoes, carrots, onions, dried peas, dried apple rings, prunes.
From garden: leeks, kail, purple sprouting broccoli, lettuce & rocket (from frames)
From wild: nettles, wild garlic, good King Henry, bishop weed (ground elder), hedge garlic, dandelion leaves.

MAY'S CHORES

- Sow carrots, beetroots, more peas, parsley, other herbs, land cress, wild rocket
- Make successive sowings of small rows of salad plants under cover.
- Hoe, and hoe again, to get on top of weed seedlings as they germinate!
- Later in month, plant out brassicas from seed rows into permanent positions, leaving plenty of space between plants. They grow very big!
- Sow courgette, cucumber & squash plants in small pots under cover. French and runner beans can also be done this way, or in tubes rolled from newspaper.
- Increased daylight shows up the smuts, dust and cobwebs from winter, so it's time for spring cleaning.
- Collect lichens for dyes and dry them for future use.

The next two weeks were taken up with sowing the great variety of seeds that I had ordered from Thomas Etty Esquire, a specialist in old varieties of vegetables. His list of things dating from about 1800 is impressive. The gardeners in the great houses of Scotland would have had access to seeds from the south. And perhaps it is possible that an enthusiastic amateur gardener in the Lowlands (maybe the dominie's wife) could have cultivated a friendship with such a professional. Then, she might have had seeds passed on to her. I had to purchase mine, however, and at £12 for the authentic seeds, and a further £40 for the routine order from the Organic Gardening catalogue, they were collectively my most expensive items of the year.

Next, I set custard marrows, pumpkins and cucumbers to germinate. A 1796 copy of the (Edinburgh!) *Herald,* given to me by Caroline, contained an advertisement for 'A treatise on the culture of the cucumber'. I had tried, and failed, to grow cucumbers in the past, but in order to keep right up to date with my period, I was determined to try again.

Also in keeping with cottage life, I was dealing frugally with an unexpected contribution to the household when visitors disturbed me. The gift was a small roe deer, culled from the Wildwood Environmental Project that I have been part of since its inception. We have to control deer numbers until the trees grow tall enough to cope with browsing, and Hugh Chalmers, the project officer, had brought me the carcass a week before. We had flayed it and left it to hang in the stable. One sunny afternoon, I decided to butcher it and salt down some joints. I had it on a table outside

the cottage when I heard voices and neighbours Brian and Pam came around the corner with two other people. I recognised the sculptor Ronnie Rae and his wife, Polly. I was, quite literally, up to my elbows in gore. This was embarrassing as both Ronnie and Polly are vegetarians. I should have trusted Ronnie to rise to the occasion, however. 'Oh Fi, you are so natural!' he boomed in his Old Testament prophet's voice, and then stayed on to watch the butchering process whilst the women retreated to the garden. By the time they returned, I had finished and cleaned up. A small deer does not take much time to dissect.

I salted down the joints and passed two of them over to a friend with a smoker. He hot-smoked one of them, making a product that was utterly delicious. The other, a haunch, was cold-smoked, and came back to hang as a ham in the airy outer space of the cottage. It was fiendishly salty, so it kept well. To use it, I shaved off a few slices and soaked them thoroughly before adding them to the pot. They flavoured many a broth more successfully than plain salted meat.

I wondered several times whether Anne Houston was ever faced with having to salt down a whole animal. It was a widespread custom to fatten a beast for winter meat and to slaughter it in the autumn. It was called a 'mart', and was usually an ox or a cow. A schoolmaster's family would probably not have owned such an animal. If they had had anything, it would have been a milk cow, but even that is unlikely, given that they usually only had a garden rather than a field. However, they may have got together with some neighbours to buy a mart and share both the labour of cutting it up and salting it down, and the benefits of having some meat for the winter months.

Some households never saw red meat at all, although a perquisite of shepherds was 'braxy'. The term now refers specifically to a gastro-intestinal illness that can kill sheep, but in the past it meant anything that died on the hill. Having seen sheep die (you can't fail to in the countryside), I found that idea nauseating, although I have butchered our own lambs in the past. All in all, I was grateful that I only had a wee quantity of venison to deal with, and that there were not so many 'umbles' (offal) that I had to make haggis. Butchers were just getting established at the end of the eighteenth century, mostly in towns, where new trades were flourishing and people had money to spend. A schoolmaster's wife, however, could only have bought bones, a little bacon and an occasional haggis on the small amount of cash that she had available to spend each week.

Late May brought another festival and some more vegetarians. It was the Traquair House Medieval Fair that had enticed a family of seven from their Angus retreat. The children, ranging in age from twelve down to three, were home-educated, lively and passionately engaged with history. Mollie, the eldest, had spent weeks making an authentic medieval gown, all hand-sewn, which she wore with great flair, turning the heads of more than the purist re-enactors. All of the others dressed up too, and I wondered whether I should scrabble around in the dressing-up box to find my wimple and gown from a museum project on the Middle Ages. Instead, I decided to stay with my chosen century, and went to the event as a sort of double anachronism.

Roe deer, and the results of my home-butchering.

The gates of Traquair House, thought to be the oldest continuously inhabited house (since 1107) in Scotland. ⟶

A carrion crow feasting on 'braxy'. ⤵

Measuring out the meal for baking bannocks.

A millstone from an eighteenth-century watermill.

The fair gave me an opportunity to mess around with different cooking techniques. I had acquired a big metal pot with legs – it wasn't a proper cauldron, but more of a Dutch oven. I'd read about baking bread in these, and thought I'd give it a try. Where bread existed in medieval Scotland, it would mostly have been 'mashlum', meaning mixed-grain bread. In towns like Peebles and Perth, bakers would have made large loaves of mixed wheat, barley and rye for such townspeople as could afford it. White wheaten bread they made solely for the rich. The great majority would have made their own bannocks and oatcakes at home because cash was in circulation even less during the Middle Ages than it was during the eighteenth century.

I had acquired coarse wheat flour from the same mill as my oatmeal and barleymeal. I didn't have rye, so I used a mixture of all three, with dried yeast because there was no time to make barm. (To do this, you have to

Thomas Bewick's drawing of a watermill and granary. →

Nettles growing behind my cottage, and delicately coloured apple blossoms in the orchard.

leave a paste of flour and water to ferment. It takes a few days and is tricky, although I remember my mother doing it during the 1950s, when she had either run out of the commercial product, or maybe, in post-war conditions, couldn't get it.) I left the dough to rise on the back of the range in the cottage and set about making a fire outside in order to heat the metal pot. I had been told that you just have to put embers in the inverted lid of a Dutch oven, but I didn't think that this would raise the temperature sufficiently, so I put the pot over the embers of a fire and prepared more glowing coals for the lid. The loaf went in on a metal plate. It came out forty minutes later, perfectly cooked on the top but scorched on the bottom. I should have trusted my informant.

One loaf wasn't enough, so I retreated to the main house and made two more large loaves, scoring crosses on the top as they used to with English 'maslin' (surely the same word as 'mashlum') loaves. Baked in the Rayburn, these were perfect. We packed them into my creel, with cheese and butter wrapped in burdock leaves. Burdock has a good, cucumber-like smell, and I

had been using its young stems as a vegetable, so I was sure that the leaves would not taint the food. To keep the packages tightly wrapped, I pulled another trick out of Patrick Cave-Browne's drawer. Years ago, he had taught me how to make nettle string (see below). The nettles from the hen yard were just tall enough to yield 18-inch stems, and the children were impressed when I showed them how to strip off the outer leaves with my bare hands and pull back the outer bark. You loosen this at the bottom of the stem, then pull it down over your thumb, letting the nettle ride up. (That way, you have more chance of getting long fibres than if you peel the stems in a conventional manner.) The bark from two or three nettles is then laid together and can either be rolled into string on a bare thigh or else be twisted in the hands in a manner that is difficult to describe, although easy to learn. Soon Callanach, the eldest boy, was adept at the process, and we had ample string for our food parcels.

NETTLE STRING

To make string from nettles, separate nettle fibres from their woody stems using exactly the same technique as described for preparing rush lights (see page 158). Now make two even-sized bundles from the fibres of a single nettle (or borrow from another if it's a skinny one). Next, knot them together at one end. Grasp the knot in your left hand and, using your right hand, separate the two bundles. Twist one bundle seven or eight times away from you. Secure it between the index finger and thumb of your left hand. Now twist the other fibre bundle away from you for the same number of turns. Hold the two bundles to the right of the twists in your right hand. Release your left hand and allow the twists to run together. Adjust your left-hand hold to a new position above the combined twists and repeat the twisting and plying operation, first with one bundle and then with the other.

Clearly, this is easier to demonstrate than describe: you can find video instructions on the Internet. Once the knack has been learned, it is easy to do. You can join new fibres into each bundle as you near the end, either knotting them or carefully laying them into a twist.

String made from very green nettle fibres tends to unravel as they dry. Dry them for a day or so before you start, and the results will be more stable. For a thicker result, repeat the operation with two of your sections of nettle string, although note that you will lose length, of course.

Nature notes

May 1st. Wet, with low cloud. Rose very early but aborted attempt to climb Lee Pen to see the sun rise. Walked in Leithen Valley instead. Bluebells coming out.

May 7th. Swallows starting to nest in the privy.

May 9th. Newly hatched orange tip butterfly near lady's smocks in garden.

May 22nd. The oaks and the ashes are coming out. They always seem to be neck and neck these days, though one cold, dry spring about 15 years ago the oaks were way behind. A particular tree on Ewan's haugh (meadow by the river) was still not in leaf in mid June. It finally greened on Ben's birthday, 26th June.

May 25th. Glorious kingcups beside Tweed.

Cowslips

A bee in bluebells

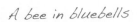

New sycamore leaves unfurling responding to the long, light days of May. These are sometimes called plane trees in Scotland.

When we came to open up the nettle-and-burdock packaging to eat our picnic, we turned into a sideshow. As we sat on the expanse of my cloak, which we'd spread over the grass, no passers-by commented on my incongruous petticoats and mobcap – they were far too intrigued by the funny little historical meal that was being consumed by our hungry rabble.

My final May houseguests (not counting my local friends, who quite frequently joined me for lunch or a meal in the evening) were members of the Incredible String Band. This group had colonised a row of cottages on a local estate back in the 1960s. In those days they had caused amazement with their hippy appearance and unheard-of ways. One member still lives in the same cottage, so he didn't stay, but five others occupied the house and used the former barn, adjacent to my cottage, for rehearsal. At last I had some music ringing through the building! Up to that point I had heard only the sound of my own singing voice (poor) and recorder-playing (worse) and one lovely recital, when friends sang madrigals for my entertainment. I was feeling musically starved and was still – even during these longer evenings – pining for the radio.

An old-time fiddler strikes up a tune.

96

CHAPTER 8
Life Outdoors

❧ JUST AS I WAS SETTLING into a thoroughly outdoor life of gardening and messing about with old-fashioned ways of doing things, the outside world was starting to make more claims on me. Work on 'The Guid Scots Diet', the museum exhibition that had been the initial spur to my project, needed revision. A steering committee had convened, and its vision was a little different from the initial brief. I resented the intrusion on my antique world, yet had no choice but to spend at least two days a week in my office, researching and writing some new text.

I still lived in the cottage, though, and dressed for the life, kept my fire going, cooked on it and entertained all but my elder son and his family out there. The start of June was chilly, and their baby was still young enough for them to have anxieties about the temperature of the cottage. Older children adored it, though, and Sam, my four-year-old godson, and his brother, Angus, were frequent visitors. They discovered a secret route into my box bed via a little door that we had left in the partition. I housed the slop pail in it, but they soon moved that and played elaborate games, worming through the small space and then commandeering the bed itself to use as a pirate ship or witch's house.

Those days when I could escape my office and become wholly cottage-based again became a pleasure – at least, when it didn't rain. I was looking forward to a fine day on which to do my washing. Although it was easy enough to wash out my sarks and linen towels and to boil up the clouts that I used for general swabbing-down purposes, I had a backlog of sheets to launder. The time had come for a proper washday. Folklore and books like *The Female Instructor* (an early manual for the young wife) abound in advice about how to conduct it. You had, for example, to start on Monday: 'They that wash on Monanday / Hae a' the week tae dry'. The later you left it in the week, the more of a slattern you were, until: 'They that wash on Setterday / Are dirty daws indeed'.

Dorothy Wordsworth, visiting Scotland in 1803, commented frequently about the dirty houses. At Leadhills, for example, '. . . the plates were on shelves, and the dish-covers hung in rows; these were very clean, but floors, passages, staircase, everything else dirty', while Burns' house in Dumfries was 'dirty about the floors as almost all Scotch houses are'. But she did praise the women whom she saw washing clothes in the burn and leaving the linen to dry and bleach in the sun. She found only one group 'indecent', but for reasons of impropriety, not hygiene, in that they were thumping out the dirt from their clothes on a tabletop tombstone in a churchyard. That seemed sensible enough to me, but it clearly offended Dorothy.

It was lovely being outdoors so much and enjoying the long, light days, even if it seemed to rain too much for me to attempt to wash the sheets. This is the view from behind my cottage.

It was not just rainy days that were holding me back from the task. I had it in mind to make soap. I understood the principles: you need tallow, and you need lye. Tallow I had already made and stored. It is rendered-down animal fat. The butcher had given me a great bag of fatty scraps that I had carried home in my creel. Hard kidney fat was the best, I found, but the process of rendering produced a reek and smoky fumes that hurt the eyes. Lye was another challenge. This is a caustic liquid that is made by soaking wood ash in soft water and then filtering it. In Scotland, they once used ferns to make the ash, ferns being a rich source of potassium, which is what reacts with the water to produce the alkaline solution that cleans the clothes. The ferns were dried and then burnt in pots over a fire, hence 'potash', which became the chemical name potassium.

I discovered a recipe for making soap that ran to several pages. The more I read, the more I felt I didn't want to go through with it, as my diary records:

I found out about soap-making: filthy, dangerous and slow! Only the people on the big estates where there was an excess of animal fat did it for themselves. Fat was too valuable in other homes, either for candle-making or else for the cooking. I went back and looked at the First Statistical Accounts, where I thought I had seen something about soap. Sure enough, in the lists of annual accounts (it's great that some of the ministers were prescient enough to supply these for a range of different households), I saw soap mentioned frequently. It was an item that was purchased, not made at home. <u>Memoirs of a Highland Lady</u> confirmed that the farmer's wife who boiled her own soap was unusual. What a relief! But I am still curious about lye.

Making lye was messy, but not difficult. The resulting brownish liquid was unappealing. It smelt like caustic soda, and I didn't fancy rinsing my sarks, or my sheets, in it. Yet before the advent of soap, it was used for boiling linen. The accounts put a heavy emphasis on rinsing – no wonder women would take the washing to the water rather than cart the water to the washing. My diaries reveal the search for the right spot in which to wash my clothes:

After supper, I walked down to the Quair to inspect a possible site for clothes-washing. The sheep-watering hole at the bottom of the glebe will do, although there are no big stones for rubbing things on. I looked around for something that I could drag into position. The nearest rocks are a long way off, and the best one is really far too far. Besides, I suspect that it is an old boundary marker, one of those stones "erected as meiths", from the description in the Kirk Session Record of 1747, when they were setting out the minister's riggs and his grazing. It would be wicked to move it, even if I could.

Heavy rinsing at the pump or in a burn was also needed when earlier cleansing agents than soap were being used, such as cow dung and 'pish' (stale urine). In 1705, when Joseph Taylor, a London lawyer, visited Edinburgh, he was astonished that the women 'put their cloaths with a little cow dung into a large tubb of water, and then plucking their petticoats up to their bellyes, get into the Tubb and dance about it to tread the cloaths'. Once soap started to be commercially produced during the late eighteenth century, cow dung, not surprisingly, fell in popularity. Urine, however, continued to be used for all manner of cleaning purposes in houses great and small.

Women washing clothes in 'tubbs' – a spectator sport in those days.

On a day when the sun finally shone and a breeze lifted the last flowers from the chestnut spikes, I stoked up the fire. My two kettles of hot water would not be enough. I made another fire outside, carrying out a candle to light it. I put a gridiron over it and set my 4-gallon pot of water on top. It heated remarkably quickly. Before long, I was lifting my petticoats up to 'my bellye' and treading my washing in my wooden washtub. I rubbed the clothes with my industrially made bar of soap, seeing it with newly appreciative eyes.

Washing clothes used to be a sociable event. In large households, it would have been tackled by several women, the servants and the mistress often working together. This went on even as late as the end of the eighteenth century. It was only the women from poorer households who used to assemble on the banks of the burn. I had gone on thinking about whether to heave the wet clothes the 150 yards downhill to the Quair Water. Yet modern farming, with its silage pits, middens and septic tanks draining into the Quair, was putting me off the idea. And once more, I lacked a companion. It would be more work to lug the clothes, pot, kettle, tub and all the rest of it all that way by myself than it would be to carry a string of buckets across the yard.

Treading the washing turned out to be fun – although I would not have wanted to do it in winter.

Mungo was all for bathing al fresco in the washtub.

Had I had the wit, I would have put my washtub near the tap. Instead, I stuck to my home ground outside the cottage door. At least the kettles were near at hand. It was there that my friends John and Rachael found me when they turned up a full hour before I had expected them. 'Wonderful,' I thought, 'another pair of hands.' I'd washed, rinsed and wrung all of the small items by then, and had even managed the first sheet. But three more sheets were still going through the process, and the last of the hot water had yet to be carried from the fire in the hen yard.

Rachael greeted me first, with Mungo (aged fifteen months) wriggling on her hip. He'd seen the water, and within seconds he was down and dabbling. One small leg was hitched over the side of the tub to join mine, then the other. We trod the sheets together. But Mungo was all for sitting on them. Soon his clothes were off him, and he was chuckling as he wallowed. Thank goodness there was no lye anywhere near his infant skin!

My hopes for an extra pair of female hands to help with the wringing faded, for babies can't be abandoned in washtubs. In the end, it was John's hands that came to the rescue. He wrung so effectively that the sheets looked like skipping ropes, and I, on the other end, was almost spun into the air. There was nothing eighteenth century about this scene. When men figure in pictures of washing from that date, they are never doing it, but are always leering at the women's legs or being chased away with the long, wooden 'beetles' that were used for beating the dirt out of the linen. Getting a glimpse of what lay below the raised petticoats was clearly irresistible to them.

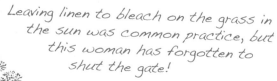

Leaving linen to bleach on the grass in the sun was common practice, but this woman has forgotten to shut the gate!

A sunny day with a breeze is great for washing, and I had my linen dry and folded before teatime. Even my woollen winter petticoats were dry enough to bring in to air. The dirt had poured out of their muddy hems, and it took four rinses for them to come clean. I had tackled them after my friends had gone, so the process had taken all day. Imagine that in the worst of winter! By running through their vast stocks of linen, the rich could have afforded to put off the process. But if the poor wanted to be clean at all, they were obliged to wash in all weathers, and to drape wet things around the house. There are accounts of children being sent naked to bed early on a Saturday evening so that their one set of clothes could be laundered ready for Sunday. What a boon the new public wash-house on Glasgow Green must have been! Its supplies of hot water impressed Dorothy Wordsworth in 1803:

> There are two very large rooms, each with a cistern in the middle for hot water, and all around the room are benches for the women to set their tubs upon. Both rooms were crowded with washers; there might be a hundred, or two, or even three, for it is not easy to form an accurate notion of so great a number... It was amusing to see so many women, arms, head and face all in motion, all busy in an ordinary household employment, when we are accustomed to see, at the most, only three or four women employed in one place. The women were very civil. I learnt from them the regulations of the house but I have forgotten the particulars. The substance of them is that 'so much' is to be paid for each tub of hot water, and 'so much' for a day, and 'so much' for the overlookers of the linen, when it is left to be bleached.

It's a shame she couldn't remember the prices.

✿ Perhaps my clean, wooden floor would have impressed Dorothy, too. Not wanting to waste my surplus lye, I used it to scrub the boards. The grease marks just disappeared, although the overall effect was not to bleach the boards, but rather to colour them slightly.

At the end of my long day of washing, I had crisp linen sheets back on the bed. What a keen pleasure it was to slip between them! The tuck-over was silky-smooth, for I had pressed it with a flat iron. 'All of this activity,' I thought, 'I have achieved on just two bowls of broth and some barley bannocks.' But then the base of the broth was rich venison stock from the bones of the deer that I had been given. For more than a week, it had turned the hungry gap into a time of feasting.

Old-fashioned soap works well when you wash by hand.

MY FOOD: JUNE

From store: last of the potatoes, carrots, onions & apple rings.

From garden: new spinach, new kail, lettuce, rocket, new potatoes & strawberries at end of month.

From wild: nettles, Good King Henry

MAKING A LEEK BED

You can make a bed in which to grow leeks as follows. From one end of the area designated for the leek bed, dig out a barrowful of earth, one spit (or spade's depth) deep and about four spits in width. Dump the earth at the other end. Fill the barrow with farmyard manure or garden compost and spread this a few inches deep over the dug patch. Now dig out the next four spits, scattering the earth to cover what you have just manured. Repeat the procedure until you reach the other end, using the initial dump of earth to fill the last section.

Next, you will need to make planting holes. These will fall in on themselves if you work with dry earth, so water the ground if necessary and leave it to stand for a few hours. Now, take a thick dibber (an old spade handle, sharpened up a little, makes an ideal one) and use it to make holes at least 8 inches deep. These should be 4 inches apart in a deep bed, or 6 inches apart in an ordinary one. Then dig up your leek seedlings (which should have been sown in a cold frame in March and should now be about 8 inches high). Drop one into each hole. When you have finished, fill the holes with water and walk away. Unless the weather is exceptionally dry, the leeks should need no further attention beyond one good weeding session.

June tumbled by. It's an intensive month for gardening, with the sowing of carrots, French beans, a second one of peas and salad stuff to be done, and lots of things to be planted out, from tender marrow plants to leeks, which require deeply dug and well manured beds. If I was not working on 'The Guid Scots Diet' exhibition, I was in the garden. Guests had to join me there, and some of them found themselves helping with the weeding. But long summer days always make me restless, and despite all of this activity, once I had handed over my first draft for the museum text, I found that I had itchy feet.

I dearly wanted to see the sea, so I started to plan a walk to the coast. I got out a map, reminding myself that it was an anachronism and that I would not be able to take it with me. The simplest route was to follow the Southern Upland Way, which passes my door and leads – not directly, but with dog-legs and diversions – all the way to the Berwickshire coast. It fell fairly naturally into a four-day walk. I had friends dotted along the way with whom I might stay for three of the nights, but the fourth was a puzzle. There is not much hay in barns in a Scottish June, nor are modern, round bales as good a prospect for a bed. Should I chance a warm night and a 'hedge bottom' (like that recommended to the dominies and ministers (see page 20) or would I have to pay for accommodation?

My friend Helen came up with a solution. She knew people who lived at the critical point in my proposed journey, and would negotiate with them for beds so that she could join me for a day's walking. Not being able to pick up the telephone, I wrote letters to all of the other households that I had in mind, and then had to wait for their replies. I hoped that receiving a curious, antique letter of folded paper, sealed with wax, would encourage people to respond quickly.

Many a traveller in earlier times was forced to rest 'in a hedge bottom'.

By that time I had got used to writing with a quill, although cutting them was still a hit-or-miss business. You need the pinion feathers from geese or other large birds, like turkeys, and a very sharp knife (see below). It helps if you harden the shanks of the feathers with hot sand, a process that I only managed once. Sometimes I cut well, and would then have a nib that lasted for weeks. At other times I was paring, and despairing, every few minutes. I noted that the poet Samuel Taylor Coleridge (1772–1834) took with him thirty-two pens (meaning quills) for a three-week trip, so he clearly got through them at quite a rate. If his paper was as rough as the authentic stuff I had acquired from an obliging mill in Ireland, I am not surprised. It looked the part, but had a surface like coarse blotting paper, and my nib scratched away over it, spluttering frequently. When I see the letters I wrote to my sister Gaie, which she kept and kindly restored to me as a further source of anecdote and recollection, I feel embarrassed: they look like a schoolchild's efforts.

QUILL PENS

To make quill pens, first select large wing feathers from a goose, turkey or similar bird. (Traditionally, only the longest three or four pinions from a wing were used.) Equip yourself with a very sharp knife – a new Stanley blade will do well. If you want to use a traditional penknife, choose a small one, sharpen the blade until it is razor keen and reserve it for this job alone.

Heat an old tin containing sand in a medium-to-hot oven for twenty minutes, remove from the oven and then plunge the quill shafts into the hot sand as far as they will go, to temper them. After a few minutes, the quills' transparent tubes should become opaque. They will feel harder and slightly more robust, because they have shrunk a little.

Use scissors to strip off the lower barbs of the feathers so that they don't get in the way when the quill is held for writing. Now hold one feather upside down and cut across the tube, up and away from you at an angle of 45°, to remove the tip. Next, pare away one side of the quill, then the other, until the nib is the width you like. Lastly, lay the quill on its back on a board and divide the tip of the nib with a single cut to allow the ink to flow down it. Try out the quill and make adjustments as necessary.

Writing with the quills took a good amount of practice — and in my case, it didn't make perfect!

Part of the problem in the early months of writing was the ink. Encouraged by my friend Roger Deakin, in Suffolk, who had been experimenting with elderberry ink, I had made a good quantity the previous autumn. It was a pretty colour of purple, but a little pale. I had to dip the pen into it frequently to have enough ink to make my writing legible. That contributed to the problem of writing fluently and sometimes caused me to drop blots. I was amazed that Gaie could read some of my epistles well enough to reply to them, but she faithfully did, writing to me almost every week of my year in the cottage. Since our usual exchange is far less frequent, it was a token of how generously she engaged with my project, and I was grateful. The arrival of the postman, usually halfway through the day here, was a moment of anticipation, and often of pleasure in the 'real' letters that I received. People take more time when they put pen to paper than they do when dashing off e-mails, and I was treated to stories, secrets and plenty of gossip to keep me going, not only from Gaie but from many other friends.

To improve my letter-writing performance, there were times in April and May, before the trees were fully in leaf, when I gathered oak apples. These woody galls from oak twigs have long been used for ink, and I had a recipe for it from an old copy of *Inquire Within*. The recipe instructed me to grind up the oak apples and boil them in an iron pot. I did this when Susie Reade was here, sketching me once again, and found an ancient, iron saucepan that had come out of a ditch. You need something rusty, for it is the interaction of the

My inkwell and a quill.

tannic acid from the oak and the iron salts from the rust that colours the ink. The mixture remains acidic, so that it makes an encaustic ink: one that cannot fade because it burns into the paper.

Susie entered into the business of ink-making. I couldn't offer her my new product, as it takes a few days before it is ready to use, but she seized upon the remains of the elderberry ink, skimmed off the curious mould that was starting to form on it (a gelatinous blob a bit like a purple yoghurt culture) and found a stick. And with the ink and the stick, she produced some dashing drawings of me, the old witch huddled over her vile brew.

The oak-apple ink turned out to be a pale brown. Somewhere, I had read of people adding lampblack to their ink to darken it, so I collected soot from a candle flame and stirred it in. The ink ended up a brownish black, and it has certainly not faded. I put it into an ancient glass inkwell and was able to use it for the rest of the year. For I went on writing my messy letters even during the light summer evenings. Being deprived of other forms of communication provides an overwhelming incentive to keep on writing.

OAK-APPLE INK

Oak apples are the brown, woody galls left on oak twigs by a particular type of wasp. They should be easy to find, so collect a pocketful of them. Crush them using a mortar and pestle (or a hammer). Put the bits, with a pint or more of water, in an old iron pan, or, failing that, in any old saucepan, but add a rusty old iron nail. Boil for twenty minutes. The ink is formed by the reaction of the tannic acid in the galls with iron sulphate. Cool and leave for a few days.

The resulting ink may look pale, but will darken over time and will leave a permanent mark on the paper. If you want to work with a darker ink, add 'lampblack', which is easily collected by catching the carbon above a candle flame on the back of a long-handled spoon or similar implement. (Take care not to burn yourself!)

MY WORK IN JUNE

- Direct sow French and runner beans, giving them some protection if possible, but making sure that they are well watered.
- Transplant courgettes etc. to permanent sites. Protect them with cloches (or fleece, or plastic, if you are living in the present!)
- Continue to make successive sowings of small rows of salad plants under cover.
- Hoe, hoe, hoe.
- Carefully hand-weed onions, as they hate root disturbance.
- Start to harvest first crops.
- Gather up long runners from cultivated brambles and tie together, out of the way. Net the bushes or the birds will eat all your fruit.
- On a hot day, pick elderflowers in the sunshine, to make wine, cordial, or 'champagne'.
- Make your leek bed (see page 106).

By June, the first of my potatoes are ready for harvesting. ⟶

Nature notes

June 4th. Bats flitting low over road as I walked this evening. Ash tree leaf-tufts looked feathery against the luminous sky.

June 11th. A fly-catchers' nest on creeper at end of cottage. They usually prefer the main house. Perhaps this is a different family?

June 22nd. Flowers round the pond are lovely: yellow flags, spearmint and the very last of the frilly pink blossoms of the bog beans. The hedges are full of wild roses.

Scottish bats illustrated by naturalist William MacGillivray, who was born during 'my' decade.

Roses and flowers by the pond.

CHAPTER 9
Midsummer

JULY CAME BLAZING IN. Milk was starting to go sour in the cottage, so I rigged up a canvas bucket of water and put the milk jug in that. Evaporation kept the milk cool enough to last for two or three days, if I was lucky. The system worked well when it was really hot and the evaporation got going, although it didn't seem to be as effective in slightly cooler weather. That left me with a problem because I couldn't just pop down to the village to buy fresh milk, which is exactly what most modern country-dwellers do, and without giving it a second thought. My green ideals have always held me back from making entirely trivial car journeys, but it is a very different experience to depend entirely upon feet.

In bad weather particularly, 3 miles is a long way to traipse to a shop, so I had avoided going down to the village much during the winter. Since then, I had fallen into a pattern of walking to the village once a week. Now, if I wanted fresh milk, I had to go twice as often.

The advantage of walking to the village so frequently was that I went on seeing things that I would have missed had I been driving: a barn owl in February, hunting by day, for example, its ginger-and-white plumage almost perfect camouflage for the snow-streaked grassland beside the river (see page 49); a goldcrest low down in a bush; or that kingfisher that I glimpsed above the burn near the Tweed (see pages 38 and 40). In March, between wild rainstorms, I had noticed the quickening of the first hedgerow plants. Elder and honeysuckle were coming into leaf, and the few surviving elm trees were bursting their buds to reveal fuzzy, red flowers, so subtle that you could only see them close to. June had brought in the wild roses, slowly at first, but then in a wonderful array of subtle pinks. Near the top of the hill was an almost white dog rose, and beside the turn-off to the mill was another, with olive-green foliage and deep-pink flowers; both appeared to be *Rosa canina*.

NATURE NOTES

July 6th. Walked up to check water supply.
There was a big eel in the intake-pool.
That's a first!
Harebells on the
bank there.

July 20th. Goldfinch
family on seedheads of
short weeds in yard.
Youngsters rounder and
lack colourful heads.

I had also been experiencing the countryside at unusual hours as I walked to visit friends. In the spring twilight, I loved travelling on foot over the hills for 2 miles for supper with friends in the glen. Walking home by moonlight was magical: owls were hooting and birch trees appeared as though they had been engraved against a pale, luminous sky with the darkness of the woods falling away and the circle of silver hills opening up around me as I emerged from the trees. Before the invention of electric lights and cars, gatherings and ceilidhs were arranged for nights when there would be a good moon. People used to wait eagerly for the publication of the calendar so that they would know when to expect these.

The old hill paths that lead over the watershed give an even better sense of what it meant to maintain social contact in the past. It takes me an hour and half to climb to the head of my friend Helen's valley, and then another hour to descend to her house. I always felt a frisson of excitement as I scrambled down the final grassy ridge. Would she be there? Once she wasn't, but fortunately other friends in her hamlet were. I should have written to make arrangements, as the Wordsworths did when they walked from Grasmere to see Coleridge in Keswick. That is a distance of 12 miles, so they would have wanted to be sure of a bed for the night.

William and Dorothy Wordsworth completed a much more ambitious walk when they made their tour of Scotland in 1803. They did have a vehicle, an 'Irish jaunting car', but the horse that pulled it was old, so most of the time he pulled the baggage while they walked. They caused a stir when they went down Peebles High Street, as Dorothy related: 'Well-dressed people were going to church. Sent the car before and walked ourselves, and while going along the main street, William was called aside in a mysterious manner by a person who gravely examined him – whether he was an Irishman or a foreigner, or whatever he was, I suppose our car was the occasion of suspicion at the time when everyone was talking of the threatened invasion.' (The French were expected to invade from Ireland at any moment!)

Dorothy was a good reporter who had a keen eye for domestic detail. Rural life in Scotland really was different from that in England, and she was quick to notice the unusual. I enjoy her observations. Over the course of my year in the past, she became something of a heroine: a woman from 'my' period who had enough spirit and freedom from social conventions to travel. Through her I learnt that the noisy inns of Scotland had box beds in their sitting rooms; that the walls of Burns' widow's parlour were painted blue; and that green umbrellas were already being used in the Highlands. I sometimes marvelled at her cheek: for instance, the Wordsworths loitered around Burns' house when the family was not at home until a maid eventually let them in for a poke about. Another time, in a tiny house near Loch Lomond, Dorothy, in her (I imagine, shrill) English voice,

demanded of her hostess, 'Why are you not using a rolling pin?' The good lady, who was patting out her bannocks with her hands, kept her silence. It suggests that she had never heard of a rolling pin, which are not items frequently encountered in museum collections relating to that period.

It was Dorothy who inspired my 'big walk'. I needed to travel light. The stitching was going on my old leather satchel, but with an extra strap, I could see that it would hold just long enough to get me over the hills. This was an exercise in how to travel light in an eighteenth-century manner, and my diary lists what I took:

a penknife;

a horn beaker;

two rags (one for washing, one, a towel);

a wooden toothbrush (Dorothy
   Wordsworth can't have used one:
   'Soon I shall have no teeth', she says,
   'but at least I am beloved.');

a comb;

a clean sark;

clean socks;

a notebook and pencil;

an Indian shawl (a pre-1900 pashmina);

an anachronistic waterproof cape;

a 'scrip (leather wallet) containing: eight
   barley bannocks, eight oatcakes (too
   crumbly!), cheese, dried apple rings
   and prunes (all of this being home
   produce, except for the cheese).

I have packed everything, even my food, in the little leather scrip that came out of Dziadzia's shed. But now I am panicking about footwear. I don't think the old leather boots will do at all. I still have problems with blisters when I wear them to the village and back. I think I must trade what looks right for what will be comfortable and wear my proper hiking boots. What about sheep ticks, too? They've not been a problem for my bare legs around the garden, but I'm paranoid about picking them up from the hill. Shall I wear leggings under my skirts? Will decide in the morning.

The waterproof cape was my one concession to the twenty-first century. In the past, people avoided travelling in the rain if they could. The famous Doctor Johnson and Mr Boswell imposed themselves on their Skye hosts for days and days while waiting for the weather to improve. Having made my arrangements, and needing to return to tend my garden, I did not have such flexibility.

In the end I did wear the hiking boots, and the leggings, with long, white kilt socks to meet them at the knees. With nasty cysts (sometimes on the brain, causing 'louping ill' in sheep) or Lyme disease being caused by ticks, I was taking no chances.

What an extraordinary four days I was embarking on! I set off in dreary conditions: the clouds were low, and it was threatening to rain. With me was Charlie Poulsen, an artist friend who had been staying on and off for a week or two as he worked on an environmental sculpture on the hill below the Minchmuir. I'd heard all about his big ellipses cut into the heather, which change when you view them from a certain place, and was eager to see them. We climbed the track to his *Point of Resolution,* and, despite the misty conditions, I experienced the pleasure of seeing the shapes on the moor magically resolve themselves into circles. What a puzzle they would have presented to eighteenth-century travellers on that stony track. These days it is probably the mountain-biking fraternity who see them most often as they hurtle through the edge of the group on one of the '7stanes' designated cycle trails.

Charlie and I parted in Galashiels, he to take the bus back to his car in Innerleithen, and I to hike the remaining mile and a half to my billet. Before he left me, we sat for a few minutes in the only café that was open.

My garden needs a lot of attention in July, from weeding to harvesting and storing.

It was dreadful: ugly, dirty, raucous and littered with the debris of half-eaten meals. We watched folk buying burgers, chewing a mouthful or two and then abandoning them. They didn't look worse than any other burgers – it's just what people seem to do, a strange by-product of an overly affluent society in which waste is of no account. We wondered whether any of the denizens of the café had ever been the 200 yards up the hill, where wonderful woodland sweeps down, to meet the town. We wondered what the folk of my decade of the eighteenth century would have made of their descendants' behaviour.

I spent that first night in an authentic corridor-bedroom of an old farmhouse. It reminded me of similar houses of my youth, where one bedroom opened out of another. Privacy was clearly much less of an issue in the past, and it is not an issue for me now, although no one actually came through the room whilst I was sleeping. Breakfast, which I enjoyed in the stone-flagged kitchen, was timeless. My hostess made porridge in my honour, so I set off well fed, and in bright sunshine. Within seconds it was raining, however. I donned my woollen shawl first, but soon gave in and wore the anachronistic waterproof cape. This got me – dry above and bedraggled below – to Melrose, and the house of other friends. I was having coffee when the news came through that Gillian Clarke, my hostess in the tower house on Easter Sunday, had just died in the hospital not half a mile from where I was sitting.

The rest of the day was claimed by Gillian's husband, Peter, who needed a companion during those dreadful hours when he was struggling to assimilate her death – long dreaded, but never wholly anticipated. Late in the afternoon,

I accepted his offer of a lift from Melrose to Lauder, where he dropped me off. It was still pouring. I trudged through parkland on the Southern Upland Way before being forced to switch to tarmac in order to make for the next house where I was expected. The road was too busy and visibility was too low, so I took off to follow a river, which seemed to be leading in the right direction. It was, but the burn meandered, and my progress over fences and dykes, crossing side streams and gullies and battling through long grass, took hours.

I have probably never been wetter in my life than I was when I reached the settlement where I was expected. This was the household of Helen's friends. I knew that their home was eccentric-looking, but had forgotten her description of it. The house sat beside a river, which was in full spate: water like strong tea rushed down, between alders and willows. The round end of the building stood on a wooden platform behind a big hawthorn. It looked as though it was just a modest hut, built of straw bales and roofed with a plastic membrane and more of the bales. I could not help but see it as a compost heap waiting to happen. 'Hippies', I thought, and mentally prepared myself for a cheerful evening of lounging around on floor cushions.

A mature hawthorn in midsummer.

S and C wash themselves with a daily dip in the burn, summer and winter alike. They have a special little shingle shore below the house and a stone for the soap. C washes the clothes there, too. They grow vegetables and say that their needs are few. But they are quitting Scotland. The hut (Aga and all) has been sold and they are off to Italy. We saw pictures of the run-down farm they are buying. S plans to fly himself there in his light aircraft; C is not so sure. What a baffling blend of simplicity and sophistication they present.

Yet when I knocked at the door, my hosts appeared, immaculately clad – he in cream moleskin knee breeches; she in Liberty-print trousers – and invited me in, out of the rain. Inside, a long, low, gallery-like building stretched away from the 'hut', which was a neat, airy, octagonal room they called 'the loggia'. The long gallery was a rhythmic stretch of bookcases and large astragalled windows, ending in an apse that was glazed rather like a showman's wagon. The furniture was elegant, the fabrics, rich; glass-fronted cabinets displayed silver and fine china; and in the centre of the kitchen space stood a cherry-red Aga. Despite external appearances, this was a gentleman's residence worthy of Dr Johnson himself. The conversation, which was scholarly and civilised, lived up to the interior. I could not have been more comfortably received as I sat in borrowed clothes whilst my own were draped and drying near the Aga.

Helen joined us, and the conversation during the evening ranged widely, eventually returning to the essential elements of a simple life. I learned that my hosts embraced it as fully, if not more fully, than I did.

The following day, walking for eight hours across the Lammermuirs, Helen and I saw only one other person. Even the village through which we passed was empty. How very different from the countryside of two hundred years ago, we observed. We trudged on to the next village, where other friends of Helen live. There we sat and stiffened up too much to be able to walk the last 3 miles to our real destination. We were rescued by John Behm in a pick-up, and were then driven back at carriage pace along a lush forest track, the very path that we should have walked along. It was good to 'ride with a carrier' after covering nearly 20 miles that day, and even better to be at rest in John and Rachael's ever-fascinating, friendly, cluttered kitchen.

I walked alone on the final day. The sun beat down on me, and my leg hurt, so I limped along. But there was a wonderful section through a long wood where I could admire creeping Jennie, marsh orchids, honeysuckle and all of the summer flowers that were in full bloom. Red admirals, ringlets and small heath butterflies flew between them; I even spotted a small copper.

I had been prepared for grey, but my first glimpse of the sea revealed it to be the brightest of blues. I sweltered along the last stretch of cliff to the little harbour, where I was expected. Outside his fisherman's cottage, my host greeted me. My son, Ben, and several mates of his joined us. We swam with the flooding tide, which came in like liquid green glass.

The next morning, there was a lobster in my host's pot, so lunch was put together rapidly and included a herby salad from the flourishing plants growing by the cottage door. I sat in the sun and scribbled a few notes. People paused in their promenades to eye me in my archaic garments, but no-one asked me why I was wearing them.

I returned home by a complicated route, which I admit did involve some modern conveyances as well as walking, only to

122

— A bright day on the Berwickshire coast.

Bold colours of midsummer: raindrops making my honeysuckle all the more vivid, and a butterfly lights on its bloom.

find that I had forgotten to buy milk. My consequent trip down to the village was less easy than usual, for like many another traveller, I had ended up with a blister. Despite it, I was glowing with the pleasure of having completed my long walk. The reason for it – to see the sea – might have been regarded as whimsical by eighteenth-century standards. Yet the people of the past did make long treks when they needed to, their prime objective usually being to visit relatives. For those separated by hills and valleys, walking the high pony tracks and drove roads was the only option. 'You should have had a horse', is what people now say to me, but the reality is that few people owned them in the past. Wheeled transport was even less common: as late as the 1770s, there were only about seven wheeled vehicles in Peeblesshire. No wonder that the Wordsworths' jaunting car caused a stir. Walking may have been a necessity for people in the past, but it had, I realised, become a necessity for me, too. I do not just mean that I had to do it for practical purposes – I had grown to delight in the slow progress from place to place. Walking time is thinking time, and I found it as beneficial for the head as for the body. Indeed, I had begun to see the absence of walking as one of the major problems of this century. If people would only get back on their feet to travel, it might counter a multitude of ills.

Gillian's death brought me a rare moment of twenty-first-century experience. I had been feeling more and more deprived of music, but suddenly I was asked to help Geoffrey Baskerville, a friend of both of us, put together the musical programme for her funeral.

That was the only time that I broke the recorded-music taboo. Twice in the year, though, I listened to the radio. One time was in order to hear Ram talking about the experience of being a trainee anaesthetist, the other, to listen to myself on 'Open Country' (see page 87). The broadcast of that programme was the occasion of the last funny story Gillian ever told me. Some two weeks before she died, her husband had taken her south to get a Norfolk terrier puppy. On the way back, they were keen to find a pub where they might pause in the car park to listen to my programme before going in for some food. They didn't know the area, so, seeing a police car in a lay-by, they stopped to ask for directions. 'I'm glad you only want to know the

Geoff brought CDs for me to listen to, so we repaired to the house. Guilt at breaking my taboo on recorded music soon evaporated with the delight in hearing 'Dido's Lament', from the Purcell opera, and Richard Strauss' Four Last Songs. Geoff thought that we should start with the former and end with the latter: a brilliant choice as the mood was set and sustained. How amazed my innocent ear was to hear high music! Afterwards, we ate a frugal supper outside the cottage door, warm in the shade, but not midged because there was a breeze. Yellow flags, foxgloves and spearmint around the pond are bringing colour to the grey yard. The swallows were chattering, and curlews, calling down the valley. We felt sad, but at ease with the evening.

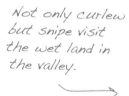

Not only curlew but snipe visit the wet land in the valley.

Foxgloves. ——→

way', said the friendly copper. 'I don't want business at the moment because I'm just about to listen to some madwoman from Scotland who thinks she is living in the eighteenth century.' He added that he had been watching a kestrel feeding on a squashed rabbit – an unusual policeman, they thought, but then Gillian always did attract unusual people.

Another unusual person arrived at my door because he had heard the same radio programme. Michael Phillips is an academic who is working on a biography of William Blake (1757–1827). He had become fascinated by the domestic life of William and his wife, Catherine, and thought that I might be able to contribute some insights. The decade I had chosen to try to recreate was the very one when Blake had lived in Lambeth, completing the poems and creating that eccentric masterpiece of hand-printing, his *Songs of Innocence and Experience*.

Michael accordingly wrote to me, and I arranged to meet him from the bus in Innerleithen. We then sweated up the hill, pausing for coffee at the Traquair House café, which was becoming a routine dropping off point for me when I was escorting visitors who were not used to walking 3 miles in one go. When we got back to the hearth, the kail pot was ready with his broth. And he was ready, too, with question after question about the practicalities of life, the daily routine, the provisioning, the struggle to find fuel, the gardening and the complications of doing it all in heavy petticoats. I was in my element answering him, and agreed to try to think about all of these things in a London context, rather than a Lowland Scottish one. I recorded the most interesting charge that he gave me (overleaf).

125

Michael Phillips wants me to create a list of vegetables that Catherine Blake might have grown in her garden. Since we know that the Blakes had a considerable plot behind their house in Lambeth, and since Catherine came from a family of market gardeners in Battersea (too far away to pop home for a bunch of radishes), it seems very likely that she did grow her own. I shall have to look back at the lists the head gardener at Clumber Park gave me, and at the earliest-dated varieties in the Thomas Etty catalogue, and at the English eighteenth-century list I have.

Occasional visitors like Michael were one of the boons of the year. My daily life, too, was cheered by the arrival of Sylvia, an artist friend from Cyprus who returns to Scotland every summer and usually stays with me. I don't think she had grasped that my sojourn in the past meant that I was not using my car, but she quickly adapted. Taxis ferried her to and from a local fishing lake, where she indulged her obsession – fly-fishing – most days. Sometimes she struggled, with her artificial knees, down to the burn that she has fished on and off for forty years, the trout that she brought back making a welcome addition to our diet. The big ones provided several feasts that we shared with neighbours, accompanied by new potatoes and fresh, young peas, and followed by strawberries – all of the best things that the summer garden was starting to provide. Small ones were consumed at breakfast, which we shared when she emerged from the main house to sit on the bench by the cottage door. Our outdoor life continued right through the summer.

Waiting for trout – or just deep in thought?

TROUT COOKED IN CLAY OVER AN OPEN FIRE

To cook the fish, you will need some string (made of nettle fibre if you are keen to be authentic!), as well as a flat stone and river clay (note that potters' clay is too refined).

- one whole trout or another fish (gutted)
- salt, pepper and herbs, such as marjoram or wild garlic, to taste
- burdock leaves

Allow one fish weighting at least 1 lb for two people. Season the fish with salt and pepper and lay some herbs in its body cavity. Wrap it in the burdock leaves, folding the leaves around the fish so that it is entirely covered. Tie up the fish package with string. On a flat stone, pat out enough clay to accommodate the length of the fish. Place the wrapped fish on it, then build up clay over it so that the top and sides are completely covered. Smooth down the clay and then place the stone beside a fire for twenty minutes to dry off a little.

When the clay seems dry, rake open the fire and gently ease the clay parcel on to the embers. Make up the fire again and keep it burning for forty minutes. Then, using sticks, carefully remove the parcel from the fire and put it down where you can safely break off the clay. It will be very hot! There should be a slightly gritty leaf parcel inside. The challenge now is to remove the protective leaves and get a perfectly clean, beautifully steamed, trout on to a plate. (It can be done!)

MY WORK IN JULY

- Go on hoeing and weeding.
- Harvest, cook and invite your friends!
- Surplus broad beans, peas and calabrese all freeze well.
- Make jam from surplus berries.
- Sow seeds of varieties of onions that will over-winter.
- Collect tall, single-stemmed nettles. Strip outer fibres from them to make nettle string.
- This is a good month for brewing beer if it's warm!

JULY: MY FOOD

From the garden: new potatoes, peas, spinach, spring cabbage, calabrese, spring onions, radishes, lettuces, rocket, broad beans, baby marrows, first small beetroots, strawberries, raspberries, cultivated brambles, gooseberries, blackcurrants, redcurrants

From the wild: first raspberries, wild strawberries

꧁ CHAPTER 10 ꧂
Fine Fowls and a Fair Gown

THE HOUSEHOLD now suddenly expanded with the arrival of two goslings. I had talked about getting geese, but these were a surprise, brought by friends. We let them out of their box in the orchard, where I have an old duck house that I thought would do for them. The goslings had other ideas, however. The fence proved no obstacle: they were still small enough to go through it, so within seconds they were following us across the garden, calling for us to wait. We put them back, but it was in vain: the goslings liked company.

We brought garden chairs to the orchard so that Sylvia and I could sit with the young birds whilst they grazed and got used to their surroundings. Names were discussed. I thought of Archie and Annabel, although there is no easy way of knowing the gender of a young goose. We decided that the bigger one, who flopped down and ate from a sitting position all of the time, was a male, and the wee one, who was fluffy and more active, must be a female.

Geese were certainly part of eighteenth-century households: they were eaten for special occasions. Indeed, my cook's eye was already appraising the two birds, although I kept silent on the matter as there were children present. I had never eaten a goose from my own back yard, but I was hoping that I would be able to do so by Christmas. The biggest of our own birds reared for the table was a Muscovy duck. In John Galt's *Annals of the Parish*, a sailor returning from the Baltic brought a Muscovy duck to a lady of the parish. It was initially viewed with suspicion, but was then accepted as being 'of the goose species only with short, bowly legs . . .', and 'was received into fellowship by the other ducks and poultry'. Galt tells of an amusing mishap to the creature: 'There happened to be a sack of beans in our stable, and Lady Macadam's hens and fowls, which were not overly fed at home, being great stravaggers for their meat . . . went in to pick, and the Muscovy, seeing a hole in the bean-sack, dabbled out a crap-full [cropful] before she was disturbed. The beans swelled on the poor bird's stomach, and her crap [crop] bellied out like the kyte of a Glasgow magistrate, until it was just a sight to be seen with its head back on its shoulders.' After a great hue and cry, the schoolmistress performed a 'Caesarian' on the bird's bulging crop, 'taking out as many beans as filled a mutchkin [about a pint] stoup'. Then 'The Muscovy went its way to the waterside, and began to swim, and was as jocund as ever.'

'Jocund' well described my pair of goslings. Their wanderings were taking them further away from us, and from the orchard. I could see them starting to eye up the young cabbages and rows of lettuces. Hens are never allowed into my vegetable garden, and I had no intention of suffering grazing geese either. After a brief fantasy about pressing the old playpen into service (could my daughter-in-law ever use it for baby Ruaridh if geese had been there first?), I realised that the birds would have to go into the hen yard. Just as in that Ayrshire parish two centuries ago, they were soon 'received into fellowship' by the hens and the guinea fowl. The only problem was that they made horrible green messes all along the path to the woodshed. The cottage floor received these second-hand, so I found myself scrubbing it more frequently. It was another chore to take me away from my writing and my garden.

Plum, one of my downy goslings – a welcome gift from friends. But I knew better than to get too sentimental about them.

You couldn't accuse this woman of being sentimental about her poultry.

Gardening in August is always a scramble. The long-tended crops suddenly bear fruit, and this time of plenty therefore brings about frantic harvesting. Peas, broad beans, kail, cabbages, turnips, beetroot, spinach, cauliflowers – everything comes at once. The first problem is how to gather the crops before they spoil, the second being what to do with them. In normal years, I freeze a good deal. In 2004 I didn't bother, knowing that I would have to do without frozen goods the following year. Nor did I think of doing so during my cottage year, when I ate only what was in season. But I did want to have a go at pickling.

When I looked closely at my old cookery books, something interesting emerged: there are very few traditional Scots recipes for pickles and preserves, although there are plenty of English ones. In *The Art of Cookery*, published by Elizabeth Taylor just over the border at Berwick in 1769, the author describes how 'to pickle . . . onions, kidney beans, red cabbage, beet-root, wall-nuts, mushrooms'. But we know that she was emulating the famous Hannah Glasse, whose own cookery book was published some twenty years earlier. Hannah wrote for the gentry, and Elizabeth, for the rich merchant families of the prosperous port of Berwick. Despite the

BLACKCURRANT KEESEL

The ripening of soft fruit is a wonderful moment if you are dependent on what is in the garden for your meals. I don't think this recipe is Scottish, nor is it from my chosen period (it's from about fifty years later, when exotic foodstuffs were more available). However, I'm including it because I love the smoothness that the tapioca gives to the blackcurrants. The keesel's texture is like that of blackcurrant jam, but it doesn't have the intense sweetness.

To serve six:
- 2 tbsp seed tapioca
- ½ pt boiling water
- ½ lb blackcurrants
- ⅓ pt cold water
- 2-3 level tbsp sugar

Scatter the tapioca into the boiling water in a pan, stirring vigorously to stop the seeds from sticking. Add the blackcurrants and the cold water. Bring back to a simmer and cook very gently for about half an hour, stirring frequently. When the tapioca seeds are clear (and not before!), stir in the sugar, then boil for a few more minutes. Cool slightly, then pour into bowls to serve.

My larder in August

From garden: new potatoes, peas, spinach, baby turnips, cabbage, new carrots, onions, spring onions, radishes, lettuces, rocket, broad beans, baby marrows, beetroots, raspberries, gooseberries, blackcurrants, cultivated brambles.

From wild: raspberries, wild cherries, first brambles, boletus mushrooms.

From top: radishes, gooseberries, mixed berries

proximity of Berwick and Lowland Scotland, people living in these two places enjoyed very different standards of living. Well-to-do households can grow a surplus, but poor ones seldom can. Nor, in the past, did they have many containers for preserves. Pots were still not a common feature of humble Scottish households during the late eighteenth century. Sending children out to pick produce from the wild was one way to fill whatever preserving vessels they could muster, and Marian McNeill's classic book, *The Scots Kitchen*, gives evidence that there was a tradition of using wild fruits. She has no pickled vegetables, though, her 'old family recipes' being for jellies of rowan, and sloe and apple, and jams of blueberry and gean (wild cherry), and of rhubarb and ginger. I was wondering how far back the jamming tradition went. It was John Galt's account for the year of 1787 that clarifies the issue and gives it a further social context.

By the opening of new roads, and the traffic thereon with carts and carriers, and by our young men that were sailors going to the Clyde, and sailing to Jamaica and the West Indies, heaps of sugar and coffee beans were brought home, while many, among the kail-stocks and cabbages in their yards, had planted grozet and berry bushes; which two things happening together, the fashion to make jam and jelly, which hitherto had been only known in the kitchens and confectionaries of the gentry, came to be introduced into the clachan.

Home-made raspberry jam on warm bannocks: very popular with my visitors!

Perhaps my ancestor, Anne, joined the jam-making set. She lived near Stranraer, where sugar might have been shipped in. If so, I hope she had better luck with grozets (gooseberries) than I usually do. And once again, they all succumbed to American mould. My blackcurrants had done better, though, so I made a little jam. Indeed, one weekend's visitors found themselves up on the hills above Traquair village, collecting blaeberries in horn beakers so that I could try Marian McNeill's recipe. But I did not get into the business of making pounds and pounds of jam because I was trying not to eat it too often. The year of limiting my diet to what was readily available demanded that I should eat less sugar, and I was only too happy to do so. Besides, the carriers to which Galt refers are no longer a feature of these parts. Sugar therefore had to be carried up the hill, and consequently had to be used sparingly. The same applied to salt. I had used up a bag full of this when I had salted down some of the roe deer that I was given, prior to getting it smoked. I then discovered that I had little left for salting runner beans, although the crop was promising to be huge. Perhaps that was all to the good: I accordingly salted down just a small crock full of runner beans, telling myself that people ate too much salt in the past. They had salt meat, salt fish and salt porridge, and the result of eating so much salt was many people dying of 'apoplexy' (possibly coronary thrombosis). With the benefits of my more advanced medical knowledge, I was certainly keen to avoid that.

Rather than salting it, I was eager to dry as much fresh produce as possible. In good years, field mushrooms abound here. They are easy to dry in the Rayburn's bottom oven, but I knew that I would have to experiment with threading them on strings above the range in the cottage. Peas and beans, which I had dried in some quantities in preparation for my year of frugality, desiccated well on the back of the range if they were spread out over a metal plate. I could only dry a small batch at a time, but it became routine to shell more than I needed for a meal and then to dry the surplus. In this way, I soon built up a store, just as I had done the year before. Whole dried peas make a good winter meal, and taste nicer than the split ones if you give them enough time to soak before cooking them.

For the time being, I was equally concerned with summer meals, however. The start of August saw fourteen people staying in the house for the Traquair Fair, and my diary records me cooking for large numbers, on and off, throughout the month.

Any surplus vegetables, I fed to the geese, who soon lost their yellow down and grew fine white feathers. It was only a few weeks before they were big enough to live in the orchard. The delay was fortunate because it gave me a chance to harvest the remainder of the soft fruits before they got to work on them. Instead, they had the immature apples to peck at, and plenty of grass. Their names changed: the female became Plum, and the male, Pudding, these names being not just descriptions of their natures, but a reminder to everyone of their ultimate fate. A cottage economy did not allow one to be sentimental about animals – I was sure of that.

At around this time, a second batch of venison appeared from the Wildwood valley, providing an opportunity for a party. During the week that it was hanging I invited some local friends, knowing that there would be several others already there. My plan was to use the primitive cooking technique of baking in a pit. We had tried it out the year before, lining a deep scoop in the earth with granite setts, then lighting two fires, one in the pit and another on top of a further spread of stones. After an hour of a good blaze, we let the fires burn out, and then had to find a way to sweep the embers and ash aside. I now used branches and did it in a frenzy, not wanting to lose a minute of the heat from the stones. We then had to lower the meat into the pit, risking burns as we slid it from a board. My skirts were a great encumbrance, so I had to kilt them inelegantly, revealing sturdy legs stuck in boots. There are plenty of images of Scottish working women kilting their skirts, although they are usually barefoot.

One of my many jars of dried peas.

Pease pudding, proving a little too irresistible!

PEASE POTTAGE

'Take pease and seethe hem fast, and couere hem til thei berst; thenne take hem up and cole hem thrugh a cloth. Take oynouns and mynce hem, and seth hem in the same sewe, and oil therewith; cast thereto sugur, salt and safroun, and seethe hem well thereafter, and serue hem forth.'

You can make a summer version of this with green peas. It cooks in minutes, rather than hours, and is a good way to use garden peas that have gone a bit floury. You can also dice and fry carrots or other vegetables to add to the pottage, which is really a thick soup.

8 oz whole dried peas, soaked overnight in cold water
12 oz onions, chopped
½ tbsp oil
a little saffron (the expensive option) or thyme or rosemary
½ tsp soft brown sugar
1 tsp sea salt
black pepper

Simmer the soaked peas for two to three hours (without salt) until they are soft and their liquid has reduced. Gently fry the chopped onions in oil until they are transparent. Add the onions to the peas. Throw in whatever herbs you please, and the sugar, and salt and pepper to taste. Serves three to four.

To stop it from burning, and to contain its juices, the meat was wrapped in bread dough. As it slumped on to the stones at the bottom of the pit, there was a smell of toast that intensified when we started to move the hot stones, one by one, from the second fire and to place them directly on top of the meat parcel. It was a tricky business requiring wooden tongs, as a shovel moved too much ash. The next job was to spread a layer of greenery over the pit in an attempt to protect the food from the soil that we then shovelled back on top as insulation. The resulting pile was left for four or five hours.

Kneading bread in the open air made a happy change from mixing up my bannock dough. I have a big wooden trough for the purpose, bought in Scotland, but plainly not made here. Dough-kneading troughs, which are a common sight in the museums of almost every other European country, are notably absent in the 'land o' cakes'. It's further evidence that bread was simply not baked here.

By early August my apples were coming along nicely. Too soon to eat them yet, though.

From bed before 7 a.m., I think, for it was at least an hour before Sylvia joined me. I've grown so used to living without a clock that I don't think too much about the time of day. After taking Ghillie out, I breakfasted on porridge with blackcurrants and went to water the garden. I found myself weeding, then harvesting. Everything is coming on fast. Cabbages, calabrese, a purple cauliflower, sugar peas, broad beans, beetroot and spinach are all ready now. It's a good thing there are lots of people coming.

Pit-baking seldom fails to produce beautiful meat, even if the outside of the dough parcel, when retrieved from the cooling mound, looks vile (someone described it as resembling a charred helmet). Inside, however, the meat is tender and moist, with the gravy running into the surrounding bread, making instant dumplings. I have tried this method of cooking meat several times and have encountered only two problems. Once, I made the dough a little too thin and lost some of those delicious juices. Another time, cooking a big joint of wild boar, I failed to put enough hot stones on the parcel. The result was that although the meat was well cooked below, the top had to be cut up and barbecued before it could be eaten. On this occasion, the process went well. With help, I transferred the hot parcel from the pit to a wooden board, and by good fortune rather than skill, I peeled back the outer crust without introducing too much ash and grit to the food. Even a vegetarian was moved to try this wild meat that had been cooked so exotically.

In between cooking big meals, I had been sewing, finding this a good occupation to take up and get on with when talking to guests. I was still busy working on my grand dress, which had slowly been coming together all year. There was a special concert coming up in Peebles, organised by the Georgian Concert Society on its annual outing from Edinburgh, and I was desperate to attend it, and to do so in style. The shape of the dress was copied from a 1795 engraving by John Kay, the Edinburgh caricaturist. It was to be made of cotton (I had wanted a printed sprigged muslin, but could only find broderie anglaise). It was white – brilliant white – and its embroidered sprigs were pretty. When I had painstakingly cut and sewn the bodice, dress and train, I tried it on. The effect was ridiculously bridal. I knew I had to change the colour. That meant consulting *Flora Celtica,* the modern compendium of Scottish plant lore, to see how to set about dyeing it.

You can extract colour from most vegetable matter. Heather, moss, dockens and lichen were all used for this in the past, as were many other plants. Almost all need a mordant to fix the colour, however, with iron being the

This month's work – August

- Continue your harvesting, freezing, jamming, bottling or salting any surplus – or simply give extra produce away.
- Lift onions as soon as they start to die back. Dry on racks or spread out in the sun (if it shines). Do not bunch or plait for permanent storage until the stems have shrivelled and gone brown.
- On warm, humid days, look out for blight (black mottled spots on leaves, followed by die-back) on your potatoes. Dig out affected plants and use the tubers soon rather than storing them.
- Sow winter salad crops under cover.
- Collect boletus mushrooms and chanterelles to dry for use in winter dishes.
- Collect good specimens of bog-rushes for rush-light and lamp wicks. Strip bark from them immediately, before they dry out (see page 155).

I enjoyed sewing and kept myself productive by doing it even when I had company.

Many mosses and lichens can be used to make natural dyes.

most commonly used, usually simply by doing the dyeing in a slightly rusty iron pot, like the one I had used for my ink (see pages 109–10). I could indeed have done that, but a friend warned me that iron gives dark shades. I wanted something subtle, so she suggested crottle, which is lichen. The dyeing technique takes us back to fundamentals yet again, for you ferment the lichen in stale urine for a few weeks and then boil it up.

Dyeing was always done in the open air. But instead of using my usual outside hearth, I lit a small fire near to the big heap of stuff waiting for a bonfire. (I thought it would be easier to have material for stoking near at hand.) A full pot of urine, well fermented, went onto a gridiron and began to heat up. The liquid was dark brown and stinking. It needed to boil, so I stoked up the fire and went off to get my precious dress. I returned to find a neighbour looking exasperated. My little fire had ignited the bonfire heap, with all of its jumble of shrub cuttings, damp leaves and rank weeds; smoke was now pouring out and blowing in sooty rags down the valley. My neighbour, a working mother who is hard-pressed to find a moment to do her washing, had all of her clothes hanging on the line. She was cross. I was apologetic. I should have checked, or supervised my fire better.

Lavender mixed with a little mint and lemon can be used to make a pink dye. Many other flowers are used in traditional natural dyes, too.

That diversion over, I took the boiling pot off the fire and set about the trial-dyeing of a scrap of cloth. A short immersion gave a milky-coffee shade. Not bad. I steeled myself, lowered in the whole dress, swirled it around with a wooden spoon and then lifted it out again. It had changed colour, but it, like the dye itself, now stank. I left it hanging from a branch and ran to fill the washtub. It was the first of many such trips with a bucket because it took a wearying number of rinses before the garment smelt fresh again. But the colour – a pale-coffee hue that was quite pleasing – was even and fast.

There were two more tasks to tackle before I was ready for the concert. First, I had to sew on to my dress a high waistband of yellow-and-gold ribbon that really did date from the eighteenth century. This was a present from a young designer friend called Lucy, who had found it in an Edinburgh antique shop. The dress was designed around that ribbon. My other task was to find appropriate transport. On such a special occasion, I thought I should arrive at the concert in a carriage, or, failing that, a trap. There are such vehicles in the neighbourhood and I made enquiries about them, but to my dismay, both equipages were busy: summer Saturdays are devoted to the serious business of weddings, not to conveying an eighteenth-century dominie's wife with aspirations to a cultural event. So I had to tramp down to the village in my everyday bodice and petticoats, stop at a friend's house to change my boots for little slippers and put on my fine dress, and then ignominiously catch the bus to town.

CRANACHAN

I only made this traditional Scots cranachan once, when someone brought me some cream during the raspberry season.

3 oz pinhead oatmeal
1/2 pt double cream
a little sugar
1 tbsp whisky
raspberries - at least a tablespoon per person

Toast the oatmeal in a heavy frying pan over a fairly high heat to brown it. Whisk the cream, sugar and whisky in a bowl until the mixture is thick, but not solid. Spoon over the raspberries and top with the toasted oatmeal. Serves four to six.

The gala occasion was worth that indignity, however. The society had hired the Secret Room in the Chambers Institution, where the walls are clad with plaster reproductions of the Alexander Frieze and sections of the Parthenon Frieze from the Elgin Marbles. Although I had worked in the room on museum projects, I had never sat and contemplated these Classical reliefs before. They made an arresting backdrop for the little chamber concert of Baroque music, which was so much what I wanted to hear. I revelled in the experience of listening to real strings, the first I had heard for so many months, and enjoyed the tea and chat afterwards. I rode back on the bus, hoping that Anne Houston had enjoyed occasional diversions of such a civilised nature. Had she lived in a city, that would have been likely, but with a home in so remote a place, I rather doubted it.

This young woman dancing at a wedding is wearing a short jacket like mine over her muslin gown.

The view behind my cottage ⌐

Nature log

August 2nd. Wild cherries, raspberries, strawberries in abundance. Cherries are tiny but very good.

August 18th. Roadside banks studded with knapweeds and nipple-wort, a pattern of pink and yellow spots.

August 19th. Martins rest in huge numbers on the church roof. It is as if they are drinking in the sun before their long haul south. Sometimes they all fly off at once, and weave patterns in the yard, traced by their white rumps.

Garden herbs & wildflowers

~ CHAPTER 11 ~
Experiments in Dairying

BY SEPTEMBER I was clinging on to the summer. The glorious days early in the month had made me savour the sweetness of outdoor life anew because, as the evenings drew in, I knew that it would not last. Not everything about the hot weather was sweet, though. One result of it, although authentic enough, was uncomfortable. The long period of warmth had favoured insects, and flies hatched and made for my cottage in squadrons. I hung up pennyroyal and other members of the mint family to discourage them, and took special care to wrap my bannock dough, butter and cheese in cloths and to stow them in the big crock with the wooden lid, well out of the way. Even so, by late summer, I could not help noticing that something always seemed to buzz out when I opened the crock.

Flies were not the only invaders either: Loki, the cat, finally decided that the cottage was the best place in the world in which to spend his sleepy days. Cats in a living room I can tolerate. In the cottage, the living room and bedroom were the same thing, and Loki thought this paradise. A cat who has never been allowed on a bed, he found that he could sneak into my box bed without my noticing. I would finally spot him and evict him. Another time, I might grab him and speak to him sternly. Finally, I chucked him right out of the cottage. Knowing he was not wanted made him determined to get back in, and a grey shadow would flash past as I opened the door in the morning. I was usually too quick for him. But it is difficult to keep doors shut during the summer, and I would later find him curled up on my pillow.

I did succeed in banishing the cat from the cottage for a few days, however. The result was a disaster, for he had left a legacy of at least one hungry cat flea, and I was bitten on the neck. I changed all of the sheets and hung out

Loki, my cat.

I'm not squeamish about insects, but I wasn't prepared to share my space with fleas. I decided to look to my herb garden for answers.

Flea repellents: feverfew (far right) and elder. Elderberries ripen in September and are good in crumbles and wine.

the blanket. But the next night, I was bitten on my ankles. I then beat the rag rug, on which both the dog and cat sometimes slept. As I was doing so, Loki must have squeezed in through a crack, for he quickly re-established himself on my bed. The battle now entered a new phase.

I consulted *Flora Celtica* for a herbal solution to my flea problem. Highlanders used bog myrtle against all manner of insects, but it doesn't grow here. Nor does fleabane. But elder and feverfew, which were also commonly used, were both in my garden. Elder smells rank – quite disgusting – but feverfew is pleasantly aromatic, so I strewed it over the floor and crunched some dried leaves into the rag rug. The cat came back, so I had to barricade the bed. The strategy worked, for if Loki was free to roam the rest of the room, his parasites seemed to prefer him, and they eventually left me alone.

My cottage industry for the month of September was cheese-making. At the start of the year, I had thought that I would get a goat, despite John Seymour's refrain that 'the only good goat is a curried one'. I had even lined up an animal I might borrow and was negotiating for the grazing that we had formerly used for our sheep. However, I then had second thoughts. In the past, there would have been a community of people keeping and milking goats, or, as was more common in southern Scotland, sheep. If someone was ill or had to be away from home for a day, there would always have been another person to take over the milking. But I was on my own. I thought about my neighbours – there was no one who, in all fairness, I might ask to deputise. It is no small thing to have to milk another person's animal twice a day, and I could think of no reciprocal service that I might perform for the one person who had some experience of animals. Knowing that I would want to go to Edinburgh to see my grandchild from time to time, and knowing that my mother-in-law was ill in hospital, I felt that I could not commit myself to looking after a goat with the consistency that good husbandry requires.

I was very proud of my home-made cheese! I also made yoghurt with the rest of my raw milk.

Instead, I tried to acquire unpasteurised milk directly from the producer. The owners of the one local dairy farm wanted to help but were nervous of falling foul of the fierce legislation governing not just the sale of milk, but its exchange. Gone are the days when you can take your can down to the farm and come back with milk warm from the cow. (I last did that on Skye about twenty years ago.) The local farm also said 'no', in case I poisoned myself, or my guests, with my cheese. Eventually, after months of asking around, I was given about six 'choppins' (the choppin, an old Scots measure, was approximately equivalent to a litre) of slightly stale organically produced milk. The gift was the result of a friend's generosity: she had persuaded a farmer's wife, many miles away, to donate it to me. The whole operation was carried out in secrecy, not even the farmer himself knowing about the illicit transaction. Who would have thought that unadulterated milk would have become a product that had to be smuggled around the country?

Some of my raw milk was used for yoghurt, for I had perfected the art of making yoghurt with any milk that I thought might 'turn'. Although yoghurt making is an ancient process, it does not seem to have been carried out in Scotland, or, indeed, in the rest of the British Isles. But yoghurt is delicious, and I decided to make it rather than waste resources. It took me a long time to force myself to do the more traditional thing and let the milk go sour to create curds and whey. I don't normally like milky things – the idea of junket, for example, disgusts me. I had also imagined that curds and whey would be sour and horrible. In fact, I found them to be good; and with my ripe Victoria plums and just a scattering of sugar, they were very good. It probably depends on when in the souring process you catch them. Friends remember with horror being given them as children, so perhaps the process was more chancy in the past, too, when it was much more difficult to keep dairying equipment scrupulously clean.

As for the real cheese, I used the greater part of the milk – about an imperial gallon (bafflingly called a 'quart' in old Scottish measures) – for making a proper 'kebbock', or hard cheese. Although I had read about the process, I had never performed it. (Indeed, the description of the curd forming had intrigued me years ago, when I read John Seymour's books on smallholding.) Now, I successfully warmed the milk to around blood heat, added my rennet and then watched as, over the course of just a few minutes, the whole pan full of milk turned solid. My diary records the process in more detail:

I have finally made some proper cheese. I re-cured the inside of the big iron pot so that I could heat the milk without fear of it being tainted. Getting the temperature right was a challenge. It meant fuelling the fire with small pieces of wood and keeping the milk moving to get it evenly warm. Is blood heat when you really can't feel the finger that has been dipped into the liquid? Or is it when you just sense it to be warm? I opted for the latter, thinking that it would cool a little as I took it from the heat and stirred in the vegetable rennet, which I bought at Real Foods. Adrian (the local butcher) is very obliging, but I don't suppose he would know how to get rennet out of a calf's stomach.

It was a thrill when the whole pan of liquid suddenly turned into rubber. It didn't look any different. But then I poked it and found that it bounced. It was just as _The Backyard Dairy Book_ describes it. Quite amazing.

I had created fine, hard curds in my re-cured pot (I had oiled it and left it over a gentle fire for hours, until the oil hardened to make a stable and waterproof layer). I then cut and strained the curds through a colander using some thin, loosely woven muslin. Quantities of whey poured through, which I managed to catch in the big pancheon that I normally used for washing up. Before using any of these utensils, I took the precaution of scalding them – I remembered that much from a demonstration that I had seen years before. I did not want to take the chance of introducing the wrong sort of bacteria. Instead, I grated in a little cheddar to give the right sort a toehold in the fermentation process.

Next, I found myself in the workshop, using a hacksaw to take the top off a large old tin in order to make a cheese press. I hadn't time to make an authentically wooden one, like the 'chessits' of former days. Having been salted and then wrapped in nettle leaves and cheesecloth, the curds went into the tin. Weights from the house's kitchen scales then went on top, causing yet more whey to drain out through the holes that I had punched in to the bottom.

But what was to be done with all that whey? One recipe I had read suggested that it was good for making oatcakes, so I went into production. The fire had to be kept going, both for the first cooking and for the toasting. Traditionally, oatcakes were only girdle-cooked on one side; the other was toasted before the fire. There are still a few surviving toasting racks to be seen in museums and antique shops. The process is also described by various writers. Even so, I had never understood why women had chosen to do it like that. The answer emerged when I started work on this large batch: it is quicker. If you turn an oatcake on the girdle, the grains that fall off it prevent it from making good contact with the metal. An uncooked cake falls flat on the girdle, but a half-cooked one does not. Rather than wait many minutes for each oatcake to cook on both sides, you can get through the process more quickly by upending it near the heat as soon as it is sufficiently cooked on one side. I had logistical problems doing this around the firebox of the range; it would have been easier with an open fire. But by spreading

Along with my nettle-wrapped cheese, here are my own oatcakes, cooked on the girdle and toasted to finish.

My larder in September

From garden: potatoes, late peas, runner beans, French beans, spinach, turnips, cabbage, carrots, onions, spring onions, radishes, lettuces, rocket, baby marrows, beetroots, cultivated brambles, Keswick codlin & Discovery apples, pears.
From wild: brambles, blaeberries, chanterelles, elderberries.

Pictured, clockwise: lettuces, peas, cabbage and elderberries.

them over the entire metal surface and moving them around, I finally had a couple of dozen good-sized oatcakes fully toasted. I soon started tasting the crumbly bits and was delighted to find that they were delicious. I had finally cracked what I had previously thought to be the impossible: I had made oatcakes as good, if not better, than the ones you can buy. It had always irked me that this was one product where I had to concede to the superiority of the commercial makers. Now I knew a method that would work, providing I had whey.

I was left with another problem, though, which was storage, for biscuit tins were not around in the 1790s. My reading again suggested a solution: I let the oatcakes cool completely, and then buried them in the oatmeal inside the big crock where I stored my supply for porridge. They would traditionally have gone into the kist, but mine had sacks in it, rather than loose meal, and the crock was more accessible. In fact, it was surprising how crisp they stayed, even two weeks later.

I looked forward to having homemade cheese to eat with my oatcakes, although, in reality, they were long gone by the time the cheese was ready. The book said I must turn my little kebbock daily for eight days before it could come out and be dried off. It seemed fine and firm when that moment came. I put it on my draining rack, which was in the prescribed 'cool, airy place', draped the whole lot with more muslin to protect it from the flies, and planned to use it for an autumn meal when the family came.

149

It had been a few weeks since I had seen my family. A long time had also passed since my trip to the coast. Summer was running out, and I wanted to complete another significant walk. Heading for Edinburgh seemed the obvious thing to do. It is 30 miles from here, but we know that fishwives could cover that distance in a day. They used to penetrate 15 miles inland from Musselburgh, each with a creel of fish on her back, and would sometimes return the same day. They were a hardy lot, these women! Pictures show them carrying their husbands on their backs from the shore to a boat drawn up in the shallows. This was to keep the men dry, so that they did not start their long days at sea with saturated woollen breeches. The women were not just strong, but powerful, too: they sold the catch, so they handled all of the family money, which made them unusual in Scottish society. And records suggest that they formed a vibrant, and ribald, section of it.

Fishwives were not the only people to take long walks, however. The Black Dwarf, a locally famous inhabitant of the Manor Valley, to the south of Peebles, at the end of the eighteenth century, is said to have thought nothing of walking to Edinburgh for an evening's conversation with his friends. I looked at the route he might have taken and decided to try it out. It meant heading over the hills from my own valley to Peebles first, travelling along the tracks and the drove road I had used in April, but it would keep me off the modern road, which was the only possible route if I chose to head directly north. I did have a peep at a map. My proposed route was more like 40 miles than 30, which seemed too far for a day, so I arranged with friends living between Peebles and Edinburgh that I would stay the night with them.

Thomas Bewick's engraving shows fishwives at the shore, apparently unconcerned by their burdens.

Nature Notes

September 3rd. Found a good place for brambles, just next to the village. The local hedgerows are useless!

September 18th. Bracken dying back has revealed badger latrine pits at the bottom of the forest ride, lots of them. It suggests quite a high population up there, though I have never found a sett.

Brambles; trees in the September mist; 'bluebells' (harebells).

❧   It was a sunny day with just a tinge of autumn in the air when I took off into the hills. The ascent to the old drove road was, as always, a slog, but one that I had already tackled several times during the year. There is one section where there seems to be no option but to stumble through deep heather, and it was only when I reached the end of this arduous part that I discovered that a new quad-bike track had been cut through it, which would have conveyed me much more comfortably to the top of the hill. I should have known about it, had I studied the hillside closely, for these tracks are becoming very notable features of hill country.

BRAMBLES & APPLES

There is no need to make a pie from brambles and apples. Just add your hedgerow pickings to apples and cook gently, adding as little sugar as you can get away with, and none if the apples are sweet enough. Blaeberries and elderberries also go well with apples, although I only match the former with the Keswick Codlin, a reliable September cooking apple, as the rest of the apple crop comes too late for blaeberries.

I strode through Peebles without shopping or chatting, pausing only at a wonderful bramble patch on the lane out beyond the caravan site. The brambles that grow in hedgerows near to home happen to be of poor quality, being of a loose-berried, acid variety, and really not worth the gathering. Here were plump and delicious ones, so I ate my fill and put some in to my horn beaker for later. They served me well, for high in the hills above Peebles, I got lost in a minor maze of waymarked paths. I had asked the way, but my informant can't have known what she was talking about, and soon I was deep in conifer woodland, miles from the main road in the bottom of the valley, which should have been a landmark. It was now mid-afternoon. I walked on and on, hoping to get clear of the trees and find a road I recognised. But time went on, and the light was fading before I finally did get to one. I turned right – east, approximately – and hoped that I was heading for Eddleston. In fact, I had overshot it, and it was only by pure good fortune that I met up with my friend Jeremy and young Angus who had walked out to meet me. I had almost had a more authentic experience than I had bargained for, having narrowly avoided being benighted in strange country and being forced to find accommodation.

The second day led me on the old carriage road over Leadburn Moor. It's a fine road, the 1805 one, well graded, and still with an excellent hard surface visible below the grass. Towards Roslin it becomes tarmac and houses spring up alongside it. I then took to the fields and found my way into the glen, to the castle, and finally to Roslin Chapel. The car park there was full of tour buses that had brought latter-day pilgrims in quest of the Holy Grail, which is purported to be immured there, according to Dan Brown's best-selling novel *The Da Vinci Code*. American and Australian visitors were quick to ask me why I was dressed in archaic costume. This happened so seldom with local people that I was happy to chat. Not that I could linger, however, for Roslin is a long way out of Edinburgh, and I had arranged a rendezvous with Ben. I found that I could not face the trek past IKEA and the other new superstores, so I skirted around them in the direction of Hillend and took myself into Edinburgh on the road leading to Morningside. It was the most tedious part of the walk, but I could see the Braid Hills and knew that I could make for them and so find my way through Sciennes' footpaths to the Meadows, avoiding more busy roads.

By four o'clock, I was at the medical school, the home of my scientist son's laboratory. He came out to drink tea in the Museum of Scotland's café, which we thought the most appropriate destination for a visitor from the past. No one raised an eyebrow at my rig-out, even though the ingrained dirt on my hands and the pervasive smell of wood smoke in my hair were more authentic accessories than most museum re-enactors can provide.

A detail of Roslin Chapel.

Two views of the River Tweed: Neidpath Castle (near Peebles) is shown in the photo above — as well as the conifer-forested hills I got lost in.

Back home again (I had returned by bus a day or two later, having had a happy, grandmotherly interlude with Ram, Charlotte and Ruaridh), I was joined by Ben and our friend Al. They had come to make the most of the last days of summer, and our shared task was to re-felt the roof of the log shed. Using modern materials, the whole process took just a day. There was some sweating and some swearing, but much hilarity. I could not help thinking how far removed the whole business was from any eighteenth-century building operation. By late afternoon, we were all so hot that we fled to the river, the boys diving into the fast-flowing section, whilst I lowered myself in more tentatively from the bank. Did any guid-wife ever chance such a thing? I suspect not, although I bet the young girls did, if they saw a chance.

SEPTEMBER'S TASKS

- Clear old pea and bean rows, either covering the ground with lawn-mowings, or other mulch, or sowing 'green manure' seeds like rye grass & clover. Try not to leave bare earth.
- As the month goes on, start to lift main crop potatoes to avoid slug damage. Give them an hour or two to dry in the sun, then store in a cool shed, using boxes or bags that exclude the light.
- Hand weed leeks.
- Collect rowan berries, crabapples and windfall apples to make jelly.
- Use dried rushes to make rush-lights.

Clockwise from top: rowan berries; rushes; a bed of growing 'green manure'.

CHAPTER 12
Lighting Up

THE WANING OF THE LIGHT during October filled me with gloom. At the start of the month I could still cook in the twilight; just a few days later, I needed a candle. During the summer, living outdoors for much of the time, I had been burning very few candles. By October I was being forcibly reminded that each winter evening would require four if I was to enjoy a reasonable level of lighting.

My understanding of 'reasonable' was generous by eighteenth-century standards. Candles then were largely homemade, using tallow, a process that was messy, long and tedious, like so many of the domestic procedures of the past. The results were carefully husbanded to ensure that they lasted through the dark months. Not even the gentry wasted them, and certainly not on children. The eight-year-old Elizabeth Grant, of Rothiemurchus, had a scolding for burning a candle for an extra hour in order to read a book. Writing in her memoirs, Elizabeth also records how she and her brother William, aged five and four respectively, were sent up to bed alone without a candle. They had to mount a great staircase and pass, on a landing, a 'big hair trunk'. This gave William the terrors each night, but it was months before their parents realised the problem and allowed the drawing-room door to stay open. Only then did the pair have a little light to see them all the way up to the top landing, where a small lamp burned.

That lamp would have been a crusie. Paraffin was not yet available, and lamps were still of the primitive boat shape that had been used since time immemorial. It would probably have burnt whale oil. I had an old crusie and wanted to try it out. This had a raised channel on which to place a wick made from the pith of a bog rush.

The ideal time to gather bog rushes is in August. Children were once sent out to cut them, and, as children will, they invented games and competitions to go with this seasonal activity. The most exciting aspect of rush-gathering

I was going to need a lot of candles to get me through the long, dark nights. That's a crusie in my hand and rush lights hanging behind me.

WICKS FOR SIMPLE LAMPS

Bog rushes also yield effective wicks for simple oil-burning lamps. Use healthy, thick, green specimens.

Make a spike or use a thin wire nail to pierce each rush a few inches from the top. Bend the top and grip it gently in your teeth. It must be firmly held, but avoid biting through it. Now use both hands to steady the point of the nail or spike as you draw it slowly and smoothly downwards, through the length of the rush. The pith should pop out at the end in a bundle, which will quickly open up into a length of wick. Dry the wick for a day or two.

Use your wick in an open, boat-shaped vessel, like an Aladdin's lamp. If you don't have such a thing, find some clay on a riverbank and fashion one. If you are not able to fire it, just dry it out in an oven and use it on a tin lid or saucer, so that the oil does not drain out and become lost.

was extracting the pith ('taking the pith', Ben quipped). This was done with a spike. You pierce the rush near the top whilst holding the tip of the plant between your teeth. You have to be gentle, because it is easy to bite through it. The spike is then pulled down, right through the centre of the rush, and if you are lucky a great bundle of pith pops out at the end. The rubbery stuff soon bounces back into shape, and people can compare how long a piece they have each extracted. It was the quest to find the greatest length that kept the children of Orkney busy at Lammas (1 August), and their games generated the bundle of wicks that would have been required for a whole winter's burning in the crusie lamps.

I had forgotten the trick for extracting the pith, so I again had to consult Patrick Cave-Browne, who had not only set me up initially with my tinderbox, but had come thereafter at intervals with new flints to replace the blunt ones. He had also gone on providing me with charred linen for tinder, so that I only once had to make my own. He additionally made candle moulds for me, and initiated me into many arcane (and smelly) processes. His letters to me to make arrangements were always hand-written with a quill, and when he came to remind me about rush wicks for lamps, he also brought equipment to help me make rush lights. His kindness to me in my experimental year, and that of his wife Mary, knew no bounds.

RUSH LIGHTS

Rush lights are an effective, and easy to make, form of emergency lighting. I don't like to be alarmist, but I do foresee times when our support systems may not be as assured as they now appear. Becoming self-sufficient in one's requirement for light may be useful one day. Paraffin candles have a poor carbon footprint, but tallow rush lights – using a waste product of the butchery process – are far greener.

To make rush lights, you will need a bag of hard, white mutton and/or beef fat (kidney fat is best), which you should be able to beg or buy from a butcher, and some common bog rushes. Put the fatty scraps into a saucepan with a good lid and slowly render them down over a low heat for several hours. This will be smelly, so if you have a permanently warm oven in a range, render the fat in that, or else put the pot in your oven when you have it on for another reason. When all of the white fat has become clear, strain it and store the fat in a vessel with a lid (tallow attracts mice, as I found to my cost!) Properly rendered and strained, tallow will keep for months, even years.

Gather the bog rushes in summer, choosing long, thick specimens. Peel most, but not all, of the bark from each. You do this by first loosening it at the bottom until you can grip the strips of bark in your right hand. Then, holding the rush upside down and loosely in your left hand, with the strips over your thumb, pull them gently downwards. The rush should ride up as the bark comes away. Practise the skill – it's easy enough to learn.

Now make yourself a simple rack. Take a piece of flat wood measuring about 16 × 1½ × ¾ inches and bang eight short nails into the wood at intervals of about 2 inches. Then find some way of suspending your rack so that it's stable when unequal weights are hung from it.

Join the tips of pairs of rushes. Melt the tallow in a tall, narrow vessel (a whisky-bottle tin set in a pan of hot water does the job well). Dip a pair of rushes into the tallow for a few seconds. Draw them out, allow them to drain for a second, and then hang them on a nail. Take another pair and do the same again. Work along the rack and return to the first pair when the eighth one is hanging up. Keep dipping the rushes in turn until you have built up a body of tallow on each. It should taper from the size of a fat pencil at the bottom to a point the size of the rush wick. Protect the surface over which you are working as drips of tallow are inevitable.

These rush lights must be burnt at an angle of 45 degrees, so you will have to devise a holder for them. See mine on the next page.

Here's a close-up of some of my rush lights hanging in the cottage. You can see the rack (instructions opposite) in the photo on page 156.

Wicks for rush lights are a little different from those required for lamps. Most of the outer skin of the rush has to be stripped off, leaving just about a fifth to support the pith. There is a technique for holding the rush loosely in one hand, grasping the ends of the outer skin and then dragging it gently down, over a thumb, causing the rush to ride up and most of its skin to be drawn off in a single process. It's exactly like stripping the fibre from nettles (see page 94), except that with rush wicks it is the core, not the outer layers, that is the object. That's the theory, at least. The practice took a little time to master, but I was eventually able to strip my own rushes.

Dipping rush lights requires a deep cylinder of melted tallow. I had to beg more fat from the butcher and once again render it down slowly in my big pan over the fire. It is always a stinky business, especially when straining it to extract the membranes and stringy bits so that you have only clean, white fat left that will keep for ages. I did not have a small, deep pan for the dipping, and was at a loss, when Patrick came up with a solution. He offered two 1-inch copper pipes, closed at the bottom and set in a block of wood; they required very little fat to fill them. I then made pairs of rush wicks and dipped one into each tube, bringing them out smartly to hang over two nails whilst the next pair went in. By the time six pairs were hanging on my rack of nails (made by Patrick, of course), the first pair was cool enough to dip again. Working outside, the tallow cooled sufficiently quickly to make good 'dips' after ten immersions in the tubes. But these had to be topped up repeatedly, so there was lots of dashing in and out of the cottage with a pan of hot tallow. I found that if I worked inside, more dippings were needed and the whole place reeked.

Rush lights burn best when inclined at an angle of 45 degrees. Patrick had made a traditional wooden holder with a thin, springy twig that clamped the rush light into place. It was an attractive, ethnic-looking object, but I found that I had to be vigilant and move the stub as soon as it neared the twig, otherwise it would have set the holder on fire.

Discoveries like that made me reflect on how constrained people must have been after dark. Once the lights were lit you were at home, in one room, and that is where you stayed. You would see whether a wick needed to be trimmed or a rush light moved up in its holder. You wouldn't go off to another room, or, if you did, you would take the light with you. I was inclined to wander off to visit a neighbour and was sometimes obliged to go to the house to work in my office for an hour or two. I liked to leave a light in the cottage, in which case a metal rush-light holder, made to a traditional design, was safer than the wooden one. A candle was better still, as it needed less attention.

Candles burn for between three and six hours, depending on the type of tallow (beef or mutton) fuelling them and the size of the wick. Patrick kindly made me two moulds, but I found production slow: candles take hours to cool in the moulds, so only two could be made at once. It was best to do this during the same session as rush-light dipping, when there was a tallow pot on the fire for some time, otherwise the heating and reheating of the fat became tedious. At least I did not have the added problem of secrecy. During the eighteenth century, candles were taxed, so moulds were hidden away and used in private in the hope that neither the excise man nor a busybody neighbour would see them.

These are my holders for the rush lights, which burn best at a 45° angle.

Filled crusie with cod-liver oil. It has burnt for 8 hours and is not empty yet. The light is tiny: about one third of a candle, so the room is very dimly lit. There are deep shadows in the corners. You can make out the table and two chairs. The third is lost in the gloom. I can't properly read or write by it. But it's enough for me to move round without bumping into things. Trying to cook by it, even when close beneath the lamp, really taxed my patience. Yet this was how most houses in Scotland were lit for generation after generation. And the eyes do accustom themselves.

Seeing, of course, is what it's all about, and I ran tests on my means of lighting. I found, for example, that I could read by the light of a modern candle, although it was easier with two. It was best if the book was nearly vertical, standing in a rack that my father had made for me forty years ago, with the candle in front of it. Reading with a tallow candle proved a little more difficult, and it was even worse by the smaller flame from a rush light. It was impossible with the light from a crusie. I tried mine out: one evening, when the fire was low, I lived by its light alone. I sat in the semidarkness that night, watching the small, but steady, flame, and thought about people in the past. They had to read by the smallest of lights, but read they did. Two hundred years ago there were many more literate folk in Scotland than in England. Meeting a series of well-read Lowland cottagers surprised Dorothy Wordsworth. Near Thornhill, for instance, she called at a turnpike house to purchase some hay, 'where there was an old man with a gray plaid over his shoulder, reading a newspaper. On the shelf lay *The Scotch Encyclopaedia, A History of England,* and some other books'. Elizabeth Grant similarly mentions some Highland saw-millers, a man and a boy, who, she noticed, would busy themselves reading the classics and geography as they waited for a log to travel through the mill. All of those Enlightenment figures, too, from Adam Smith and David Hume, the sons of lairds, to the poets Robert Burns and Robert Fergusson, both from poorer homes, would have had to spend many months of the year reading by candlelight, rush light or crusie. It's easy to overlook what a challenge this represented, and my admiration for those who succeeded in educating themselves in such taxing conditions grew and grew. I myself could never read for more than half an hour at a stretch without having to stop and rest my eyes.

161

And we forget that the fire made a significant contribution to lighting a room as well. It became a winter pleasure of mine to take away the girdle and pot and let the flames climb a little. The flickering light chased away any inner gloom of my own, as well as the darkness in the room. Reading the Border ballads one night, I shuddered to think of the dreadful pledge made by Margaret at the end of the 'Clerk Saunders' ballad. Her lover having been killed by her brothers, she swears:

> There'll nae a coat gae ta ma back,
> There'll nae a camb gae thro ma hair,
> There'll neither fire nor candle-licht
> Shine in ma bour, evermair.

With that in my mind, I was grateful for my good stock of tallow candles and rush lights with which to light my bower, and for the beeswax, and even the paraffin-wax candles brought by friends. Someone had also kindly brought a whole bag of tea lights. I had used them during the early part of the year, when I had nothing else to light, but had since forgotten them.

On Halloween, I had a friend staying. We sat at the round table in the cottage and invented our own ceremony for the evening. Starting with

Tallow candles burn with a smaller flame than modern ones.

I stoked up my fire with these bellows to gain more light, as well as warmth.

It's clear from this fireside scene that the fire was an important light source and focal point as well as providing warmth, and heat for cooking.

just a single rush light, we took it in turns to light a tea light. Beginning with our childhoods, as we lit each short candle, we recalled a significant person in our life who had died. The process was anything but thrifty but the illumination was glorious by the end of the evening. We then drank a dram and let all of the spirits that we had summoned fade. The experience had been powerful.

Perhaps it was a good thing that my bedtime reading was not one of the household favourites in eighteenth-century Scotland. A book called *Satan's Invisible World Discovered proving that there are Devils, Spirits, Witches, and Apparitions* appears on many household inventories of the time. Nor did I read the ballads last thing at night, for they are too full of murder and misery. My taste was certainly not for the biblical commentaries and concordances that were commonplace in homes either. I had a copy of John Bunyan's *The Pilgrim's Progress* on my shelves as a gesture towards that genre, however, and I did try to spend time with writers of the period. Yet thoughts of tackling David Hume and Adam Smith in depth, as I had declared that I would do, faded when I discovered how difficult it was to read by candlelight. Instead, I frequently compromised and read novels. Some, like Sir Walter Scott's *St Ronan's Well* (1823), were compelling because of the local references. Others, by Jane Austen, the Brontës and Charles Dickens, all of them slightly later than my period, still kept me in the right mode. They depict a world that is more similar to that of pre-Industrial Revolution times than it is to our own. That I could not bring myself to be more serious-minded made me feel feeble. But, tired after all my hard graft, deprived of the radio and being forced to sit up with my candle rather than recline with a reading lamp, I needed comfortable literature.

Nature notes

October 12th. A very wet day: a toad appeared in the scullery. Surely it's time it hibernated?

October 13th. Mushrooms! The whole of Ewan's 'hospital field' is littered with them.

October 17th. Collected crabapples from hedge near Traquair house. There are three distinct varieties and two types of wild pear in a single hedge. Was it planted by some traveller who had visited Kazakhstan (the home of wild apples) a hundred years or more ago?

Daytime in early October, if short, was cheerful. The weather was warm and frequently sunny. Field mushrooms, which had been few in August, sprouted in legions in a south-facing field, and we had jolly weekends when visitors came and gathered basketsful. We ate them meal after meal. Ben made pints of mushroom soup, and still there were more. For days the cottage was festooned with strings of drying mushrooms.

Then the shooting season started, and Ram came home with pheasants. It did not make sense to struggle to pluck them by candlelight, as I lacked an oven in which to roast them. Instead, we skinned them so that they could go into the kail pot before we once again enjoyed their rich, gamey flavour. I found an eighteenth-century recipe that used white wine, lemon and mace, which made a pungent dish, quite different from the red-wine-based casseroles that I would previously have cooked. I did not stop to ask whether a schoolmaster's family would have had any white wine at all, let alone any to spare for the pot – my preoccupation with getting it wrong was dwindling.

BOILED PHEASANT

Browning the pheasant and onion first is a modern refinement. The original eighteenth-century recipe for boiled pheasant simply has you simmer everything except the lemon juice in a pot, but insists that you skim off the resulting scum. Pre-frying removes this necessity.

1 pheasant for every four people
one onion, roughly chopped
butter
1/2 bottle white wine
a few blades of mace
nutmeg to taste
a few cloves
flour or cornflour for thickening gravy
rind and juice of one lemon
salt and pepper
a little sugar (optional)

Brown the pheasant and onion in a little butter. Add the wine, mace, nutmeg and cloves and cook on a low heat for about an hour, or longer in a slow oven, with the pheasant resting upside down. Check that the bird is done by making sure its juices run clear; remove it from the pot and keep warm. Thicken the gravy with flour or cornflour, adding the lemon rind and juice and seasoning, adding a little sugar if you like.

SCOTCH PHEASANT – The chutney makes the gravy rich and fruity.

one pheasant for every four people
two to three onions, roughly chopped
a little butter
water

1/2 bottle red wine
flour for thickening (optional)
two big spoonfuls chutney
salt and pepper

Proceed as for the recipe above, adding chutney with the red wine and enough water to cover the pheasant. Cook slowly. You can reduce the stock after you have removed the cooked bird from the pot, and can then either thicken it or leave it clear if you prefer, as well as season it.

So, alas, were my spirits when my visitors went away and I was left to the dark nights, and the thought of the longer, darker, colder ones to come. I began to wish the year over with. The garden, with most of its crops having been harvested, was looking dejected. I pulled out old beanstalks and the weed-infested remains of pea rows, trying to tidy it up before winter set in, but apart from the shortening days, that did not seem to be happening. The air was unseasonably warm, and, despite the odd downpour, dry, too.

Now, with little warning, I found myself having to make full use of every warm and sunny moment. 'The Guid Scots Diet' exhibition was moving into its production stage, with the display boards being about to be assembled. Funds were short, and some photography had to be done on a very tight budget. There were mutterings that it would be impossible to show cooked food. Desperate to ensure that a full range of cooking from all periods would figure on those display boards, I offered to do the cooking for free. It would mean stepping out of my eighteenth-century role for a day or two, but then that was exactly what my flagging spirits needed. We found a young photographer, Malcolm Benzie, who was prepared to work to a tight budget. I had to drive my car to Edinburgh to fetch him and his equipment, stopping to buy the few bits of the good Scots diet that I could not supply myself. So it was that a big joint of beef went into the car, along with some kippers, mussels, cream and curious stuff for the wartime shots, like corned beef and shop jam. Most extraordinarily of all for an innocent from a time warp, I had to buy a whole batch of lurid sweets and snack food, which we needed for the illustration on the board describing the evils of the contemporary diet.

Autumn sunlight catching the leaves on the drenched hedgerows after a downpour.

Acorns and other edible nuts can be gathered in October.

OCTOBER'S LARDER

From garden: turnips, swedes, parsnips, leeks, carrots, kale, red cabbage, apples.

From wild: field mushrooms, elderberries, crabapples.

From store: potatoes, onions, marrows, custard marrows.

GAME SOUP

Any giblets from birds, carcasses of roast fowl, bones from joints that have been removed so that the meat can be stewed, or leftovers from stews can be converted into game soup. If I have a patently old pheasant, it certainly goes into the pot.

For the stock: 4 pints water; one old pheasant, or some combination of the above-mentioned bits of game; one bay leaf; six peppercorns; salt to taste

Add all of the ingredients to a large pan, bring to the boil and simmer for a couple of hours, removing the meat from any bones as soon as it will conveniently come away and then saving it to add later.

For the soup:
two carrots, chopped
two onions, chopped
one white turnip, or a section of a neep
butter, duck fat or olive oil
two potatoes
a little sherry, port or elderberry wine
salt and pepper

Soften the carrots, onions and neep in the fat or oil for a few minutes, and then add the potatoes. Strain the stock before adding the vegetables to it, bringing it to the boil and simmering until they are tender. Before serving, add any reserved meat (diced) and a little alcohol. Season to taste.

Leek and Oatmeal (or Leek and Potato) Soup

four (about ½ lb) stout leeks, well chopped
one medium-sized onion, well chopped
butter
2 pt water or light stock
three large potatoes or 3 tbsp pinhead oatmeal
salt and pepper
small amount milk

Gently soften the leeks and onion in the butter, without browning them. Add the water or stock. If you are using potatoes, bring to the boil, dice and add the potatoes and then simmer just long enough to cook them. If you are using oatmeal to thicken the soup, you will need to give it twenty minutes' simmering time. Mash the potatoes, or blend the soup, season, and finally add a little milk. Serves six to eight people.

'Apple Stew'

My first independent attempt at cooking was in an old saucepan over a garden campfire, using windfall apples. I must have been about eight.
'Apple stew' is what my friend and I called our watery mixture as we ate it, several times a week throughout a series of autumns. This recipe follows our simple approach, as the apples are not peeled, although it has grown a few sophistications over the years. It's a wonderful way to use up baskets of miscellaneous windfall.

- about 2 lb cooking apples, chopped, but unpeeled
- a little lemon zest
- cinnamon or cloves to taste
- white wine, cider or sherry
- a little sugar to taste

Place all of the ingredients, apart from the sugar, in a heavy pan, bring to the boil and then simmer gently, stirring regularly to prevent the apples from sticking. When the apples are cooked, but some of the pieces still retain their shape, stir in a little sugar if needed. This will depend on the varieties of apple that you use. (It's much more interesting if you vary them, rather than sticking to Bramleys.)

Our Stone Age hearth, with locally hunted and foraged fare.

The work commanded two days of preparation and two days of photography. I thought I had prepared well, but it was a real scramble to get from one antique set to the next. The Stone Age hunters' hearth was a triumph. By total coincidence, a shooting friend had turned up with a brace of mallard just before I set it up. The mallard lay before the fire, where I had secured a pigeon on a spit. Mussels sat in old scallop shells to show that shellfish was a significant element of the Mesolithic diet. There were elderberries, blaeberries and hazelnuts, too. All had been gathered locally, just as they would have been six thousand and more years ago.

We worked our way through the Roman kitchen, the medieval cooking pot, the bowls of porridge – both ancient and modern – and the frugal wartime table. And we displayed the choicest foods – smoked salmon, beef, a range of vegetables, raspberries and cream – first raw, and then as the different courses of a cooked meal. Towards the end of the second day, there was just one epoch left to be portrayed. I had yet another small roe deer that I needed to roast on a spit to represent an Iron Age feast. I had the animal ready, but it had been hanging for more than a week. It was getting high, and the flies were descending in swarms.

COCKYLEEKIE

One of Scotland's classic soups, cockieleekie, is spelt 'cockyleekie' in older recipes. I have so few cockerels that I often use pheasants as the basis of the soup and cook it for a shorter time than is traditional.

- one large cockerel or two pheasants (plus giblets)
- 4 pt water
- 1½ lb leeks, finely chopped
- 1 bay leaf
- 2 oz groats (whole oat grains) or long-grain brown rice
- 4 oz prunes (optional)
- butter
- salt and pepper

Simmer the birds in the water with 1 lb of the leeks and the bay leaf, retaining the rest of the leeks for a later stage. After about an hour, or when they are tender, remove the birds and set them aside. Add the groats or rice and the prunes, if you are using them, to the pan and return it to the heat for half an hour. Now soften the remaining leeks in a little butter in a separate pan and add them to the groats or rice about five minutes before the end of the cooking time. You can either remove the meat from the carcasses, dice it and then add it to the soup or else serve the fowl at a different meal (as was traditionally done). Serves eight.

Just as we moved from some interior shots to get the fire blazing for this final one, the skies opened, and the rain came down in torrents. A fire was quite out of the question. So was photography. All I could do was simply climb into the car again and take Malcolm and his cameras back to Edinburgh. Hours later, when I got home, I still had the problem of the over-ripe venison to cope with. Taking the creature down from its hook in the stable, I saw that it was so small that, cut in two, it would fit into the Rayburn's oven. There was no choice, so I fired up the machine, cut through the animal's tiny waist and crammed it in to roast.

I was still not sure how I would take the missing photograph, when serendipity came to the rescue. Susie, the artist who sketched me, who usually brought just charcoal or pencils, arrived the next day with her camera as the sun obligingly shone. So I made my fire, found a metal rod for a spit and reunited the two halves of the deer so that we could photograph it. That job done, cottage life could be resumed in peace.

Once I had climbed back into my petticoats, we celebrated by cooking the broth on our outside fire, toasting the bannocks on stones in a most primitive manner and drinking the last of the elderflower wine.

SCOTCH BROTH

Scotland is renowned for its broth. At its most basic, it traditionally consisted of boiled pot barley (whole grains), to which kail, 'plucked very fine', was added near the end of the cooking time. A richer soup had neeps added, and other vegetables went into the pot when they were available. On Sundays, a bone might be used to give flavour to the stock. Stories of a single marrowbone being passed around several households in a Glasgow close are hard for us to believe, but people really were poor. This recipe is for a far richer household, for a mutton flank would be beyond the purchasing power of most country-dwellers, or, indeed, most factory-workers, in the early nineteenth century.

½ lb pot (or pearl) barley
½ lb flank mutton
½ lb dried peas, soaked overnight
three leeks
three carrots
one large turnip or small swede

bunch of curly kail or one small Savoy cabbage, in either case finely shredded
2 tbsp salt (the traditional, but excessive, amount!)
parsley, chopped, to taste

Boil the barley with the mutton flank and the soaked peas for at least an hour. (Do not add salt at this stage as it can toughen the peas.) Next, add the root vegetables (diced). Cook for a further half hour, or until the vegetables have softened. Finally, add the shredded kail or cabbage and cook for a further few minutes. In the past, the meat would have been removed when cooked and used for a different meal.

Today, it is best to take it out, remove any bones, chop the meat and then return it to the pot before serving. Add salt cautiously, to taste. Use the chopped parsley as a garnish. Serves six to eight.

MY CHORES IN OCTOBER

- Harvest carrots and store in bins of sand.
- Harvest apples and store, preferably on shelves. Try to protect them from mice: wrapping each one in newspaper helps.
- As supply of mulch decreases, cover ground where crops have been lifted with old carpet, preferably old, wool, hessian-backed carpet, to keep the weeds down and stop winter erosion.
- Store canes, poles and pea sticks in tidy bundles, under cover if possible.
- Collect crabapples and make jelly.
- Collect ripe elderberries (earlier in the south) and make wine.
- Continue candle making.

Healthy carrot leaves

Fully ripe elderberries

Crabapple jelly ⟶

CHAPTER 13
Fighting the Winter Blues

AT TIMES, the sight of the cottage by candlelight could still enchant me. I went on enjoying the baking of bannocks and I made sure of keeping a good pot of broth on the fire. But delights that I had previously enjoyed throughout the year were now wearing thin.

I must have been naïve not to realise that this would be a very public way of life. I expected it for a month or two at the start, but people's curiosity hasn't waned. Almost every day brings a knock at the door (I never did get the tirling pin I wanted). Those who haven't seen the cottage realise that time is running out. Other people who have been before just want to know how I'm getting on. I love it, but today it made me impatient to have to sit in the cottage and share tea with virtual strangers when I was bursting to get outside and garden.

In some respects, the constant visitors make for a very authentic eighteenth-century experience. Life was lived more communally then, with neighbours in and out of each other's houses. I find myself sometimes falling into the mindset of a real guid-wife: Is the floor swept? Are the windows clean? Is there something to offer? Despite these prim concerns, I have been getting more lackadaisical about climbing into my skirts. No day has actually gone by without me wearing them, but sometimes the afternoon is well established before I put them on. I've been caught out in my jeans a few times now, like I was when Martin Murphy showed up the other day. I really feel that I had let him down because of his letters exhorting me 'not to let standards slip'. I must get back into my old regime for these last few weeks of the year.

NATURE NOTES

November 4th. A big skein of geese flew over in thick cloud. I never saw them, but heard their eerie calls for some minutes as they passed.

November 9th. A small bird of prey flew off from the roadside hedge. A merlin?

November 20th. On Cademuir ridge in deep frost the tall grasses were bending towards each other, swathed in white: almost like old-fashioned stooks.

Well, I did force myself to conform to most of the rules that I had set myself. And life became even more public because I allowed two local papers to come and record my year. I felt that I owed an explanation to all of the people who had seen me walking on the road or going about my business in town. I was not sure whether they had any clue what I was doing, or whether they had written me off as being barmy. The reporter from *The Peeblesshire News* hired himself an eighteenth-century outfit so that he could interview me, and be photographed with me, in style. With a double-page spread in that paper, and a page of photographs in another, I consequently lost much of my carefully guarded anonymity. People would stop me in the street for a chat, their response being overwhelmingly friendly and supportive. They cannot have been aware of how important their approbation was at a time when I was contemplating stopping the experiment before the year was over.

The extraordinary autumn also helped. It really did seem 'as if warm days should never cease' (to paraphrase Keats), so some of my anxieties about the cold and the dark were allayed for the time being. The result was that I threw myself into whatever needed to be done.

It was a surprise to find myself harvesting elderberries in early November. There they were, in a nearby hedgerow, in thick, purple clusters like bunches of tiny grapes. In previous years, they had seldom even ripened before being taken by redwings and fieldfares. I went straight into wine production. The previous autumn, I had collected berries from further afield in early October, and had used an old recipe for spiced elderberry wine. The result had been strong and sweet, something between port and mulled wine, so the drink was a real winter warmer to be shared with visitors. 'Gather them when they are full ripe... then bruise them with your hands', the recipe says. It also tells you to add some raisins and spices, but does not mention yeast, although I had introduced some. In the cottage, I wanted to make it without using that modern wine yeast, however, for it was a challenge to see whether I could induce fermentation from the natural yeast on the berries. I had tried it successfully in June with elderflowers, which are well known to have their own yeasts. Primitive people seem to have used them to make a brew, residues of which have been identified in beakers from Bronze Age barrows. How they made it ferment without sugar to feed the yeast, I am not sure. I did add sugar, and was pleased when the fermentation started. The liquid then fizzed away for weeks, turning out a palatable drink, which we consumed eagerly. Experts point out that we were fortunate: wild yeasts could well generate the wrong sort of alcohol, so it is safer to use a modern, purpose-designed one.

I had enough elderberries to be able to conduct a trial. I pulled the fruits from the stems with a fork, squashed them in the prescribed manner and divided the mush between two pails. Both were given the same mix of spices and sugar, but one of these I seeded with commercial yeast and the other, I did not. This time – probably because the temperature in the cottage was lower – only the commercial yeast got going, but even that one did not fizz in the required manner. I had to move both pails to the house, where I now had the Rayburn ticking over at a low level. Exposed to greater warmth, the sluggish brew soon started to work more strongly, but I struggled in vain to seed the other one. To save wasting it, I eventually reheated it to pasteurise it, cooled it and then started again using commercial yeast. Having tinkered with them so inauthentically, I next transferred both brews to modern demijohns with airlocks and left them in the warmest place that I could find. The recipe said they would be ready by Christmas.

176

MY NOVEMBER LARDER

From garden: swedes, parsnips,
leeks, kale, winter cabbage,
red cabbage, sprouts
From store: potatoes, onions,
carrots, marrows, apples
From wild: late elderberries.

Red cabbage.

Picking sprouts.

With winter festivities in mind, I had also been brewing beer. The everyday drink in the eighteenth century, at least before tea displaced it, was small beer. That was a second brewing taken from the mash after ale had been made. For festivals there would have been the nut-brown ale itself. I tried my hand at making both. The mash for the small beer came from a local brewery, where I had been invited to help myself before it was carted away for compost. When I was passing the door in late October, I noticed a steaming heap of mash that had just been turned out. I filled my creel with the hot and fragrant stuff. (I like the brewing smell, although some don't.) Adding my own dried hops, a little sugar and some barm made of baking yeast, I soon got the mash brewing again. It fermented actively for a few days before I strained it through muslin and bottled it. I got the moment right, for when we came to drink it a week or two later, the beer had a little head and some sparkle to help it go down. The taste was yeasty but pleasant.

That was just beginner's luck, for neither my nut-brown ale, brewed with an inauthentic jar of malt, nor my second attempt at small beer worked well. The former simply wouldn't ferment; the latter was sluggish when it did. Slightly cooler temperatures probably accounted for this, although an Edinburgh cookery book, dating from 1755, that I had just been reading recommended brewing during the winter months. That left me mystified: all of my brewing efforts of both wine and beer had depended for their success on a warm atmosphere.

Then there was the more delicate matter of the Christmas geese. After my brave words in August about cottagers not being able to afford to be sentimental, I had grown rather fond of Plum and Pudding. Plum was a freak. Her feathers developed into soft plumes that flopped around her and ruffled as she walked.

She looked like a goose crossed with an angel. I felt that she could not go into the pot. Pudding had grown strong on his legs, and was always leading his lady everywhere, immensely curious to know what was going on. With most of my crops having been harvested, I decided to give them the run of the garden. The two of them would stand beside me when I was digging, turning their heads in unison to watch every spadeful of earth as I moved it.

One fine morning in the autumn, I gave tea to two young girls, Evie and Ertha. They had seen the new film of *Pride and Prejudice* and wanted to wear their homemade, Empire-line gowns to meet me. I couldn't disappoint them by wearing my homely weeds in my cottage, so I put on my grand muslin dress and shawl, brought my kettle and tea caddy into the house and boiled the kettle on the drawing-room fire. As we sat around an occasional table, sipping tea from bone china, the geese spotted us through the bay window, mounted the outside steps and stood, peering in at us. The girls were young enough to throw off their drawing-room manners. In a trice they were out, racing around the lawn, gowns and shawls trailing in the wet grass. The geese rushed up and down, wings open, loving every minute. At that moment, I felt that their reprieve was certain. I would have to seek a new home for those geese, for my plans to travel in the New Year were starting to form. Hens are easy to leave on self-feed systems, but geese require daily attention. They would have to move on.

Ertha is only six, but she wanted to chop sticks. Sarah said, "Let her. She knows how to do it". With misgivings, I set her up in the woodshed with a chopping block and my favourite little axe. Evie came and made bannocks. I nervously flitted to and fro across the yard, but all was well. Ertha really did know what to do. She heeded my advice to keep both hands on the axe and chopped quite a pile of kindling. They both enjoyed lunch in the cottage. Lots of questions! I had to demonstrate the tinderbox, which always frightens me in front of children in case specks of flint fly in the wrong direction. But how good it is to know that there are still families where children are trusted to do a job. I told them they would have been a credit to an eighteenth-century dominie's family. I should have remembered the story of the schoolmaster of Traquair, who upset parents by making his pupils do all his domestic chores. They wrote a letter of complaint to the laird about their children being required 'to chop sticks and gather fairns for the theeking (ferns, or probably bracken, for the thatch). What a long distance from practical realities we have travelled in two hundred years. Not many kids do so much as wash up these days.

Evie and Ertha were great guests. Their mother, Sarah, took the opportunity to read a book whilst they worked.

Days like that were ones to store in my memory and recall when November turned nasty. And at times the rain came down so heavily that I felt as though we were paying for the warm days early in the month. I had sympathy for the gloom of the old woman in Alastair Reid's poem *Scotland*, when she responds to the poet's elation about the sunshine with 'We'll pay for it! We'll pay for it! We'll pay for it!' Puddles formed in the yard, and my path to the log shed grew muddy. The world took on the depressed tones of winter: the darkening browns of saturated heaps of leaves, the bonfire's grey ashes turning black, the hills inky, or lost in lowering cloud. I clung on tightly to the thought that I only had a few weeks to go, but I increasingly hated being in the cottage in the evenings.

The last November leaves.

179

These small brushes made of twigs made practical gifts. I made cloth bags filled with dried herbs as gifts, too.

❧ My self-help for this antipathy was to go out visiting. I regularly showed up at my neighbour's, Ishy's. Earlier in the year I had taken sewing round to do it in her house so that I could enjoy some comfort and conversation. Now that I had no more hand-sewing to do, I was at a loose end. It occurred to me, more slowly than it should have done, that work would be the real cure for my malaise. I would make Christmas presents for everyone!

My new purpose sent me up the hill on the first dry day. I took a sharp knife with which to cut heather and a creel in which to carry it home. A patch of woody, but nearly dead, heather offered me what I was looking for: it had long parallel shoots rather than the usual fuzzy growth, ideal for the bristles of little heather brushes. I hacked at it with the knife with little reward – I'd brought the wrong tool. Luckily, I had sneaked the secateurs into the creel, too. We do take these modern tools for granted. They enable the unskilled to carry out all sorts of tasks that would have demanded long practice in the past.

The heather, bound tightly into small bundles and trimmed (again with the secateurs – standards were slipping), made brushes that I was pleased with. One was pressed into service to replace the more sloppily made twig one that I had been using for washing up for several months. The rest were hidden away for Christmas.

I had a supply of calico that I hadn't used. That would make cloth shopping bags, I thought. It was easy to cut these out in the cottage, but suddenly, faced with twelve of them to stitch, I balked. One dark night when the rain was pouring down again and my gloom was as oppressive as the weather, I took the lot into the house and got out the sewing machine. I was tempted to turn on the radio, but did not succumb – it felt wicked enough to be resorting to Singer's excellent technology. I sat there, thinking about the huge difference that this machine had made to women's lives. Before its advent, the burden of stitching every item in the family's wardrobe, from infant clothes to table linen and sheets, fell on them. In around 1730, Lady Elphinstone is reported to have been in the habit of sitting up in bed each morning. There she would cut out the material for shirts, one for each of the daughters that she had at home that day to sew up. By bedtime, those shirts were expected to be finished. How astonishing! It had taken me days to sew a sark, and my stitching is big and untidy in comparison to the tight, neat stitches that were expected of women in the past.

When I considered that, and then the added toil of carding and spinning wool, both of which I had tried with only limited success, I marvelled afresh. Equally daunting were the endless number of tasks involved in getting flax to the point when it could be spun. In the early years of the eighteenth century, Lady Grisel Baillie, who lived at Mellerstain in the Borders, recorded in her account books her frequent exhortations to her servants to get on with their spinning. Her housekeeper was instructed to keep laundry maids, the dairymaid, housemaids and kitchen maids busy with spinning when they had no other occupation. At that date they would have been hand-spinning with a distaff; spinning wheels did not come in until the 1730s. It took until 1760 for these simple devices to become common throughout most of Scotland, and even then they were unknown in parts of the Highlands and Islands. A wheel produced four times the volume of spun yarn in a given time than a distaff, so it was a great advance. Greater still were the industrial machines

THE MONTH'S WORK – November

- Tidy up the garden, putting dead stems of courgettes, beans and calabrese on compost heap.
- Order a load of manure (or bring it in bags) and spread it on deep beds. It, too, can act as a mulch, and works even better under carpet (see October). During the winter the worms pull most of it underground, leaving a lovely, humous-rich soil.
- Now is the time to do structural work like making new deep beds, changing paths, or digging a pond.

My garden looks quite flattened in November, except for the leek bed.

The mills at New Lanark.

Spinning by hand with a distaff.

that started to appear in the first mills, as in New Lanark. When yarn could be bought, or when homespun yarn could be sent to a mill for weaving – that other occupation that was so time-consuming – women must surely have experienced the start of some real liberation. It interested me that Maggie Tulliver's mother in George Eliot's *The Mill on the Floss* reminisces about sending her homespun linen thread to be woven into sheets for her trousseau. Faced by the bailiffs removing all of her napery, along with the rest of her household goods, she is shown grieving for that more than anything.

It is another fictional character that supplies the best Scots anecdote about linen. Mrs MacClarty, from Elizabeth Hamilton's *The Cottagers of Glenburnie* (1822), remarks: 'We're no sic fools as to put our napery to use! I have a dozen tablecloths in that press, thirty years old, that were never laid upon a table!' Judging by the unblemished state in which similar napery has come down the centuries, it never did see use on a table. But such a conceit cannot have been commonplace in poorer homes before the Industrial Revolution. The labour of doing all by hand would surely have been too much for women to have completed more than they actually needed for their own family use.

As for me, the labour of stitching twelve bags with cheerfully coloured handles by machine was enough to keep me busy for several nights running. When they were done, I spent another night or two in the warmth and the light, making smaller cloth bags for dried herbs. I had a surplus of camomile, peppermint and lime blossoms, which were destined to make other little gifts. In my eagerness to muster enough home produce for Christmas, I had ceased to worry about these odd evasions of cottage routine.

CHAPTER 14
The Final Mile

MY GUILT ABOUT not doing the job properly did linger, even though I was not cheating on the essentials. I still cooked my meals from my own produce, lay down on the lumpy straw bed that I had grown to loathe and rose in the dim light of the winter dawns to make my solitary porridge. I still walked everywhere, and I did make myself wear my habit. For I was feeling more and more like a nun – or, perhaps, a prisoner, counting the days until my release.

To do penance for some of those evenings I spent in the warm kitchen of the house, I planned a slightly punishing walk. It would be good to look down on the valley from a different place. What would it be like to negotiate paths and tracks, the field and woodland, rather than the roadways, in winter? My planned destination was only the village, but my route was eccentric. One morning, when a dull rime frost gripped the ground, I took off cross-country, travelling in a circle around the hills to the east. I climbed the long field beside the Curly Burn, passing the ruined footings of Shillinglaw. The earthworks of the medieval peel tower sport a great ash tree that must date to the building's desertion during the eighteenth century. Humps and bumps extend into the next field. You can make out the defensive barmkin wall, small enclosures that must be fields, and down below the tower footings, a distinct area of flat, deliberately terraced ground. Surely that was the kail yard.

Not far beyond Shillinglaw, as a strip of wood dips towards the Damhead Valley, there are more old enclosures. They include a rectangular stone one that has within it another drystane building. Fifteen years ago this still had a thatched roof and was known to the then farmer as 'the lamb house'.

A deep frost, with the December sun shining palely at its long, low angle, picking out the frozen grasses.

NATURE NOTES

December 1st. A most unwelcome bit of wildlife has reared its head in one of the house windows: dry rot!

December 24th. The woodland trees in frost don't need any Christmas decoration: nature has done it already.

December 29th. Saw the hint of a salmon's fin in the Quair. The 'run' is on.

When I compare the enclosures with pictures in history books, I form the impression that the building would have started life as a bucht. Buchts were places where sheep were brought to be milked. If you called the 'yowes fro' the knowes' in summertime, you put them in a bucht so that you could share their milk with their lambs. One enclosure within another would have been necessary so that the old ladies could be separated from their lambs for the duration of the milking.

Dead leaves, not sheep, filled the pens in December. I descended the hill and encountered my first obstacle: where I was expecting a footbridge over a burn, there was no longer any sign of one. As a result of the rain of the previous few days, the water was high. Not wanting to hike right down to the road bridge, I wandered upstream a little and found a willow that had fallen across the burn. Inwardly praising the growing habits of the crack willow, which spreads itself by falling over and sprouting afresh from its prostrate stem, I groped my way across. It was a precarious route. I hung on to the willow's suckers and squeezed through thick growths of them, finding my petticoats an encumbrance.

Once uphill again, running through the old quarry wood was a good track that delivered me past generations of farm rubbish, collapsed machines from the nineteenth century, old tyres, rotting wellies and even, like some sentimental birthday card, a rusty kettle containing a bird's nest. Beyond the high field into which I emerged, another wood beckoned. Negotiating first the dyke, and then the wood, proved difficult. The trees concealed a great ravine I had to skirt around, fighting through a thick undergrowth of young ash saplings, until I found myself crossing the Minchmuir Road, the very track that I had followed on my route to the sea (see pages 116–120).

The low sun struggled out of the clouds at the same time as I emerged from the wood. It cast long shadows across the fields and picked out the circle of black cattle eating from a 'heck' (the local name for those metal containers used to keep circular bales of hay of the ground, though 'heck' used just to mean hay) on the muddy hillside across the valley. At that distance the beasts reminded me of the fruit baked into the top of a Christmas cake. I now had a choice of route: I could go uphill and find a forest track to take me around the hilly contours towards the Tweed, or I could go through the

Lichen-covered hawthorne and winter berries.

A seedhead captured in ice.

Long shadows on the frosted fields.

fields. I compromised and made my way to the head dyke, the wall that separates the in-bye (fenced and improved fields) from what would have been hill-grazing. The latter is now forestry land. My objective was two stretches of oak wood that I had been viewing at a distance for more than twenty years, but had never visited. Here they were at last, their top branches, shaggy with lichen, catching a lemony light from the winter sun. Below them was a surprise: a clump of aspen. This native poplar – a pretty tree that waves its long-stemmed, wavy-edged leaves at you in the slightest breeze – is now uncommon in Scotland. It hangs on in the odd cleuch and enclosure where animals cannot browse on it. It was the estate's wall around its policy woodland that had afforded this group some protection.

A track was discernible above the oak wood. I fought through brambles to gain access to it and then ascended a steep section of designated cycle path. This was part of a fearsome mountain-bike track that takes the young and rash doglegging down the most precipitous paths. Pleased not to be encountering any wild mountain-bikers, I reached the forestry track and followed a much more comfortable route for a mile or more. I had no idea where I should leave it in order to plunge down towards the Tweed, though. Eventually, recognising some birch woodland lower down, I found a path that led through a clear-felled area. This then petered out, leaving me obliged to jump, climb and beat my way through piles of old brash (brushwood) and fallen logs until I met some overgrown pasture alongside a burn. From there, it was an easy descent through a landscape I must have skirted in the past, but which I had never seen before. Hawthorns and birch trees were sprouting everywhere; grass was giving way to gorse and broom: this neglected field was turning back into woodland. The close husbandry of the past would never have countenanced such a thing.

The Tweed was the next barrier. I had not expected a problem as I knew that there was an old railway bridge crossing it. Not having driven that way for so long, however, I had not observed that this was being restored for use as a foot and cycle bridge. The girders were all there, but the sleepers had been removed. Replacing them was a teetering catwalk that stopped some 6 feet short of the first girder to prevent idiots like me from attempting to cross. Well, I was not to be deterred! I kilted up my soggy skirts and, clinging on to the steel sides of the bridge, edged my way along a ledge adjoining the catwalk. Once on the boards, it was a heady walk across the flood. My adrenaline was rushing and so was I, grateful that there was no sign of any workmen to call a halt to my wild dash across the river.

I made it! A final half-mile of an old railway track brought me to the village. It was lunchtime. I tumbled into a café and ordered some soup. A walk that would have taken forty-five minutes on the road had gobbled up two-and-a-half hours. The exercise had been vigorous, and my appetite now matched it. I looked at a framed map of the area on the café's wall and felt proud that I knew every hill, every wood and every track in my home's neighbourhood. Who, these days, can say the same? Farmers patrol their own land. Walkers stick to paths. Dog-walkers have their habitual routes. Few people ever range over the whole of a district. Even in towns, many will ride rather than walk and experience the place street by street. It felt good to have so increased my familiarity with my immediate landscape that I had

Crossing the Tweed without a bridge required agility and ingenuity. I felt the old railway bridge offered quite enough adventure for me.

a sense of its present, its past and their interconnectedness, and also of its secret places, of the haunts of the birds and beasts, and now of several more of its most interesting trees, too.

After bragging about this special knowledge to some old chaps whom I met on the lane near the mill a week or two later, I had to eat humble pie. They knew every path, and had climbed every hill, in the district. Even if old age obliged them to stick to the tarmac, they still had that very understanding that I was claiming as being unique to me. And they were still out walking on a daily basis.

During the weeks when I had been busying myself preparing for Christmas, I had given little thought to whether I should be celebrating it at all. Only in the middle of December did I start to read about the history of Christmas in Scotland. John Knox, the austere founder of the Presbyterian Church, banned it during the 1580s because of its Papist associations. His laws were only repealed in 1958, when Christmas Day became a holiday in Scotland for the first time in 375 years.

Not that the ban on the 'daft days' of Yule was wholly successful. In many places, the celebrations merely went underground, with the old customs still being observed, just not in public. In Catholic and Episcopalian areas, especially in the Highlands, the baking of the Christmas gudebread (raisin bannocks, shortbread or gingerbread), carolling and the acting of plays, or guising, still went on openly. Some even celebrated twice. The Gregorian calendar having been adopted by the Privy Council in Scotland on 1 January 1600, two centuries later some households were still observing festivals according to the old calendar. As a child in the first decade of the nineteenth century, Elizabeth Grant of Rothiemurchus and her family went to friends for the official Christmas and New Year. They then 'went home for the passing of our Christmas time – Old Style – the season of greatest gaiety in the Highlands. It was kept by rejoicings and merry makings amongst friends, no religious services being performed on any day but Sunday.'

189

If John Knox prevailed more over churches than homes in the Highlands, his influence was more generally, and sternly, felt in the Covenanting south-west. Galloway is where my ancestors, Anne and William Houston, lived. She, being English, would have looked forward to Christmas, and I can imagine her dismay when she realised that there could be no preparations for it. Even New Year would have been brought in sedately there. Yet they must have had at least something to offer New Year callers, for first-footing traditions were strong. I took comfort in the thought of the elderberry wine that I had to offer, and hoped for Anne's sake that her Protestant household in the south-west had had something like it.

I was debating with myself what I could do about a yule log. The custom of bringing home an especially good oak log for Christmas was once common in some parts of Scotland. I had seen a 1937 photograph of a Perthshire farmer loading his yule log on to a sledge for his pony to drag home through the snow. But a big log can only be burned on an open fire. Grates and ranges were not designed for wood, which I knew only too well, being obliged to chop my wood small enough to burn in a coal grate. The idea of the yule log had a certain thrill for me. It really is a remnant of pagan customs. It was lit with a glowing faggot saved from the previous year's log, 'an echo of the sanctity of the sacred fire', as the Scottish anthropologist James Frazer says in *The Golden Bough* (1890). In some parts of the Highlands, the log was carved into the figure of the Cailleach, or 'Old Woman', a spirit of winter. She was placed ceremoniously in the centre of the fire whilst the family drank ale and joked. The Covenanters would not have liked that!

My answer emerged soon enough: I would not need a yule log, for I had been invited to join Jane and Martin in the Lake District for Christmas Day. Ben and Caroline would be here for Christmas Eve, the *Wigilia,* which we always celebrate with due ceremony in memory of my Polish husband, Andy. They would drive me over the next morning, they said. The prospect of going was just too tempting, and I accepted, promising myself that I would come back on Boxing Day to see out the last few days of the year in my cottage. After all, setting aside the modern means of travel, I could think of no more appropriate place in which to celebrate Christmas than that remote farmhouse, which has avoided most of the refinements of the last century, including electricity. Since Jane and Martin had been the very first people to sit and eat at my table in the cottage (in January; see page 30), it would be appropriate to sit and enjoy their excellent hospitality at theirs, in England, for the Christmas of this extraordinary year.

There was a week to go before that happened, however, and I still had much to do. There was a feast to prepare for the winter solstice, the day I had chosen to invite some of the friends who had helped and supported me through the year. Before that, I had to file copy with *The Herald* for my final article, which was due to appear between Christmas and New Year. I launched it with a boast about how healthy I had been all year. What folly! My diary records the hubris that came hot on the heels of that boast.

Only the owls can have seen me flit: a comic figure, wrapped in shawls and doubled up. It was in the small hours last night, frosty and moonlit outside. Having kept fighting fit all year, the gripes hit me. I'd had two days of a grumbling stomach, which I put down to some dodgy smoked mackerel that Ben had bequeathed to me. Suddenly it erupted, and I fled for warmth, light and sanitation.

I have been trying to rest on the kitchen settle between episodes of my digestive drama, but cannot sleep. I keep on thinking how horrible it would have been in the past to have had a tummy upset like mine. Feverish, then frozen by the wind, did Anne Houston have to drag herself out to an ash midden at the bottom of the garden? Or was it a bucket in the cottage? Squalid, and lacking all privacy. The shakes brought on by my malady have turned into deep shudders at the thought. Some aspects of life have most definitely improved in the last two hundred years.

I have absolutely had enough of reading by candlelight and scratching away at my letters with a quill. I am fed up of having permanently grimy hands and bruised shins from chopping and heaving wood, and of never being warm. I am so relieved that I shall not have to do another major wash by hand. I'm itching to travel freely, without a sense of guilt.

Yet for all of these gripes (physical and theoretical), there were many good things that I started to consider, too. I had loved having to use my ingenuity – and not money – to find solutions to problems. It had started in January, with my stick-built draining rack, which still worked well. Along the way, I had made and mended and learnt all manner of new processes, including making oak-gall ink, quill-cutting, dyeing with lichen, spinning, making rag rugs, brewing and even some simple joinery. The curtain that I had just stitched out of a borrowed length of Harris tweed was the last item in this succession of problems solved. It was helping to block the icy draughts from the north-western window, so as I sat at my little round table in the candlelight, sipping rosemary tea, I was finally feeling a bit more snug. By then, I was assiduously wearing all of my petticoats – they were absolutely necessary for survival.

I liked living on my own resources. I had not crossed the threshold of a single supermarket that year. Nor had I bought a single manufactured food product (unless you count kippers, oatmeal and barleymeal), and I had purchased only very few basic ingredients. I had done without chocolate, bananas, exotic fruit and imported vegetables, and largely without coffee, too, although I had bought it for friends and had taken the occasional cup. Yet I had eaten well, with plenty of variety, using my own produce alone. Indeed, I seem to have eaten masses, yet was a whole stone lighter at the end of the year than I had

DECEMBER'S SUPPLIES

From garden: swedes, parsnips, leeks, kale, cabbages, sprouts.

From store: potatoes, onions, carrots, beetroot (saved for Christmas), dried peas & beans, apples.

A string of onions in my cottage, and a snail helping itself to my Christmas sprouts.

BAKED APPLES

Core some apples and stuff their centres with raisins, nuts and a little honey, mincemeat, jam or – my current favourite – two teaspoons of marmalade mixed with a generous teaspoon of ground coriander. (Coriander has a long history, and may have been used in Scotland by the Romans, or even by the Celts. It was taken to America by the first colonists, which suggests that it may have lived on in many European cultures before being rediscovered in Britain during the 1970s.)

Bake the apples for half an hour or so in a moderate oven. Not having one in the cottage, I managed to achieve the same effect by putting them in a heavy pan with just a little water in the bottom, covering them with a lid and simmering them very slowly. This worked well enough.

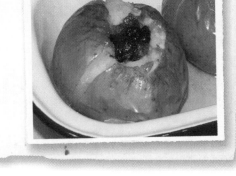

been at the beginning. I also felt more vigorous and strong. Cottage life was so physical that I had seldom sat down for long. There was simply no time in which to seize up. I leapt up to do jobs. I strode down to the village to get my meagre supplies in the shortest possible time. Deprived of my walk, my family said that I was as restless as an unexercised dog.

The touchstone for the whole project had been my work on 'The Guid Scots Diet'. I had been obliged to find time all year in which to continue with the research for the exhibition. It was seeing clearly how supermarkets have made us into passive dependents that had fired me to revert to the 1790s. I wanted to discover what experiencing the mostly self-sufficient life of the past felt like. In food terms, it had been easy. My garden had fed me and my visitors. Apart from the goodies that I had received from guests, I had bought only dairy products and a tiny range of occasional luxuries, lemons, bacon, one or two haggis and a few smoked fish. English apples became an exception in the autumn – the 2005 crop was so bad that I allowed myself that concession. Having been without apples from May until September, I could not bear to go without when they were in season.

Some of my vegetables suffered during the poor growing season.

That apple problem highlights an uncomfortable reality about the past. I had started on my year in the knowledge that I had a sound store of produce. But while 2004 had been a good growing season, 2005 was too dry. As a result my leeks were spindly, my cabbages were small, my carrots (which I would normally have protected with horticultural fleece) had fly, and even my onions were rotting. Only my potatoes were first rate. Had I been dependent on what I had managed to store by December 2005 to get me through until June the next year, I would not have starved. My diet would simply have been reduced to porridge, bannocks, potatoes and kail, with few other vegetables with which to vary the ingredients in the broth.

There were many disastrous years in the eighteenth century when crops really failed. In 1782, tradesmen in a neighbouring parish were forced to sell their tools in order to buy food. In 1795, 1799 and 1800, the heritors (the richer people in the parish) had to buy in supplies of grain with which to eke out poor harvests in the Tweed Valley. I laud self-sufficiency, but in the unforgiving climate of Scotland, it carried great risks.

James Hutton (1726–97), who is known as the 'father of British geology', toiled away in the middle of the eighteenth century to tame and improve a Berwickshire farm. He described it as 'a cursed country where one has to shape everything out of a block and to block everything out of a rock' and found himself 'already more than half transformed into a brute'. At times, groping around in the dark to find my tinderbox and candle, or trying to find papers in a kist, or wrestling to smooth out the runrig-like behaviour of my beastly straw mattress, I shared his sentiments.

Hutton was about as far as I ventured into the Scottish Enlightenment, and I never did get to grips with Hume and Smith, as I had hoped. Instead of following lines of abstract thought, I was preoccupied with practical things. I read journals and travellers' accounts and found myself trawling fiction for domestic details. It became more fascinating for me to know what Jane Austen's Elizabeth Bennett had for dinner (*Pride and Prejudice* was written in 1812, so its world was not so very far away in date) than to understand the state of her heart.

VENISON SOKEY

Lacking an oven, I could not finish off this dish (whose recipe I took from my antique cookery book) very well in the cottage, but it is well worth including here.

For the stew, for six people:
- small haunch roe deer, cut into thick steaks, or stewing venison
- two onions, roughly chopped
- ½ bottle white wine or cider
- two strips lemon rind
- mace to taste

For the crust:
- 4 oz breadcrumbs
- grated lemon rind
- dried herbs
- a little white wine or cider to moisten the mixture

Brown the meat and onions in a heavy pot. Add the rest of the ingredients and slow-cook, either on the hob (at a heat lower than a simmer) or in a slow oven for three or four hours. When the meat is just tender, transfer it to a wide dish, one layer deep. Mix and then sprinkle over the ingredients for the crust and place the dish in a moderately hot oven for twenty minutes, or until the crumbs have browned.

For the sauce and garnish:
- flour or barleymeal for thickening
- salt and pepper
- sugar (optional)
- parsley for garnishing

Use the gravy from the meat to make a sauce, adding the desired thickening agent and adjusting the seasoning, perhaps adding half a teaspoon of sugar. Serve the meat on its baking platter, garnished with parsley, and pass around the sauce in a jug or sauceboat.

OATMEAL PUDDING

This oatmeal pudding is a surprisingly good variation on a steamed pudding. It can be made in either a cloth or a basin, and is much lighter than a suet pudding. This quantity serves four to six.

2 pt water
½ lb currants or mixed fruit
2 oz sugar
lemon rind
cinnamon
nutmeg
ground cloves
brandy
6 oz medium or pinhead oatmeal (or a combination)

Bring the water to the boil and stir in the rest of the ingredients to your taste, adding the oatmeal last to make a thick paste. Turn into a well-buttered basin and cover tightly with foil or greaseproof paper tied on with string. Place basin in a saucepan of hot water and boil for about an hour. Turn pudding out carefully onto a warm dish.

December's Chores

Forget gardening and plan festive menus around your home-grown produce, from garden and store.

Continue with home-made gifts.

The birds might need extra food.

So how did I celebrate my return to the twenty-first century? Well, first there was the winter-solstice lunch party that I held on 21 December. I raided Elizabeth Cleland's *New and Easy Method of Cookery* (published in Edinburgh in 1755) for a recipe, then I raided the freezer. There was no other choice but to resort to the freezer as I could still not face slaughtering a goose and no successful hunters had passed through recently. I got out a good joint of red deer and spared a little of the elderberry wine for its marinade. I then made it into a pot roast, cooking it slowly on the side of the range at the same time as I was cooking an oatmeal pudding. This simple recipe (which came from the same book as the one for the venison pot roast), which was full of spices and dried fruit, turned out well. ('Very good!', as the recipes themselves so often assert.) Vegetables presented no problem: there were leeks and kail, and plenty of potatoes to soak up the gravy.

Then there was the Hogmanay party. I decorated the door of the cottage with holly, whose spikes were once thought to keep away evil fairies. We started out in there, nearly thirty of us, crammed on benches around the walls. I could not find a fiddler, so we had to rely on our own entertainment: everyone had to sing, recite or tell a story. I had imagined that there would be some divining, which seems to have been a major preoccupation of young girls in the past, all of them wanting to know who their future husbands would be. But we were a more mature crew, all pleased to do a turn. My sister sang a jaunty little song, some neighbours, a catch. Others read poems or bits of history. Al, my trusty roof-mender, performed a piece by Ian Dury, reminding me about a whole world that I had forgotten, not just for the year, but for many years before it. I served bannocks and broth with ale (not my own) and whisky, of course. Just before midnight, when a friend was in the middle of an intriguing speech that embraced James Hutton and other Enlightenment figures, I had to absent myself: I had four minutes in which to do a reverse Cinderella act. In my bedroom, I shed my cottage clothes, hastily let down my hair (which I had *shampooed* in preparation) and donned a slinky outfit that I had found in a charity shop the previous day. I was just descending the house's stairs when Ram's traditional New Year rocket went up, after which my guests crowded out of the damp night into the hall below. I was once again in the light and the warmth, with music, champagne and some more elegant food.

It was only the next morning, when the guests had departed, that I started to wonder how soon the car would corrupt me after this year of travelling on foot (and by bus). And how much I would miss the tranquillity of candlelit evenings; my simple interior, with its comparatively few possessions; and being outdoors so often. But, as *The Herald* reporter commented when he interviewed me in the December of the previous year (see page 22), my real house is archaic enough. I don't have a designer kitchen; I was back on the stone flags and working at a farmhouse table. But there was light, music and the wonderful, warm and convenient (although unecologically sound, oil-fired) Rayburn.

✎ CHAPTER 15 ✎
Greening Up

FOUR YEARS HAVE NOW PASSED since I emerged from my cottage purdah. I generally look back with enthusiasm on the time that I spent out of ordinary society, so that the impatience that I find recorded in the final months of my diary surprises me. Yet I can still feel my sense of liberation at not being confined. My first diary entry of the year 2006 tells all about it:

> *Kirkbride, February 2006*
>
> *Woke with the alarm (!) to see Ram off as he had to work a twenty-four-hour shift. Went back to bed, but did not sleep. Enjoyed watching the light grow on the hills above the Glen, jackdaws flocking, sunlight on the patches of remaining snow. Wonderful to be warm, comfortable, and seeing the waking world, after the confined box of my bed.*

That particular pleasure stays with me, just as my delight at living in this beautiful place has not waned in twenty-six years, but rather grows greater as I appreciate more and more how fortunate and privileged I am to be here.

Several wild and ferociously cold winters since the experiment ended have brought back to me with some force what it was like to live in the cottage during the coldest months:

> *27 December 2006*
>
> *It's twelve months since my year in the past ended. I came into the kitchen a moment ago. Outside, it is dreich, damp and the temperature hovers around freezing. Here, it's warm and cheerful. As I ran hot water from the tap just now, I remembered how it was to rely on a black kettle. It's so easy to scrub the parsnips that I brought in, so easy to cook them without all of the bother of coaxing and feeding a fire. The memory of how chilly it was comes back to me. Even right beside that cooking fire, it was cold. I am absurdly grateful to be warm.*

It's lovely to be able to choose to be outdoors but still retreat inside when it's too dark or damp to enjoy it.

People still ask whether I miss it all. In the cold and wet weather, I don't! My gratitude for not being weighed down with multiple shawls and wrappings, none of them waterproof, overwhelms any regrets about no longer living the life of the past. It was such a trial to dry out the bottom of my cloak and my saturated skirts that I avoided going out in costume in wet weather. I am sure that our forebears must have tried to do the same. I delight in being able to have a bath and to slip into a bed that has a down duvet and a sprung mattress. I delight in listening to the radio, and in letting opera boom out from the CD-player (Richard Strauss' *Der Rosenkavalier* is playing at this very moment). I even take pleasure in answering the telephone and in using e-mail. Living without these instant forms of communication was one of my biggest challenges.

It was also a challenge that, I have to confess, I did not fully live up to. I was honourable enough for the first couple of months, using my computer only to write and send off copy to *The Herald.* (I had discussed the possibility of filing my copy in longhand, and they had laughed.) Then I had to write an article for a magazine. That kept me at my desk for a day or more. At around the same time, I was obliged to start communicating with the Museum Service about the 'Guid Scots Diet' project. And some of my friends were getting a bit cross because they had made long journeys to see me and had then failed to find me at home. I began to see grumpy e-mails that they had sent to complain about my absence. Perhaps I had been in the village at the time, or maybe in a neighbour's house. It seemed such a nuisance for them – and such a loss for me – that these visits had failed. I made up my mind to concede that we would use e-mail, but only for communication regarding plans.

That seems simple enough, but it was a significant intrusion on my attempt to recreate the feeling of the past. During those early weeks, but for postal communications, I was cut off. I seldom knew who, if anybody, would turn up. Most of all, I had a very different sense of time. It was like a reversion to childhood; time moved more slowly because there was less going on. I waited for weekends when it was likely that friends would appear. I waited for the postman. I had to generate as many new activities for myself as possible in order to combat the day-to-day tedium. Opening the door to cyberspace, even just a crack, changed all of that. It was a compromise that I regret in some ways, although I also acknowledge that it helped to keep me sane.

Had I had resisted it, I would, perhaps, have developed a better understanding of the eighteenth-century world outlook. However, since I was not completely restricted to the books that would have been commonly read at the time, and since I was ducking out of church-going – that mainstay of Scottish village society – this seems unlikely. To have turned up each Sunday would have been disingenuous. Besides, I could not bring myself to compromise my atheism and go to church, even though there is one next door. I was also rather thankful that we live in a sufficiently tolerant society these days for my failure to attend not to be an issue with my neighbours. Social control, causing you to conform with your neighbours' expectations, was a very potent force in the past. I could not reinvent that. Nor could I miraculously take the surrounding world back two centuries to keep me company.

As it was, I read the newspapers of the time that Caroline had so kindly, and painstakingly, photocopied for my use at the start of the year. I noted the contemporary concerns with the Colonies, with trade, and just a little with politics. Yet I never succeeded in thinking like an eighteenth-century person. Nor could I keep the events of the decade – like the opening of the

'Hutton's Unconformity', an unusual rock formation identified by pioneering geologist James Hutton at Inchbonny, Jedburgh.

Forth–Clyde Canal in 1790; the trial of the Scottish radical, Thomas Muir, in 1793; or the death of James Hutton in 1797 – in my mind as though they were actually happening in the time frame that I was trying to occupy. I suspect that I would not even have read Hutton's words when he published his *Theory of the Earth* in 1785. Few people did, for Hutton was prolix and obscure in his writing, and it took his friend and commentator, John Playfair (1748–1819), who produced a revised and condensed version of his *Theory* a decade later, to make his work at all popular.

My other big concession to modern life was a little more travelling around than is apparent from reading the chapters of this record. I am accurate about my first trip away from home, when I caught the bus to Edinburgh to see my grandson (see page 59). After that, other obligations crowded in on me. I had to interview the artist about whom I was to write the magazine article, which entailed a car trip to Perthshire and a night with friends. I took my archaic clothes and put them on when I got there. This gave me the opportunity to answer their door to some bed-and-breakfast guests with a curtsey and a 'The mistress will see you upstairs', a comic turn that amused, but did not fool, the guests.

As months went by, there were other trips. I had to conduct another interview with an artist. Then my mother-in-law fell ill in a nursing home in Devon. I went to see her in March, and had to go again in July, when the whole of the Scottish contingent of the family – I, Ben, Ram, Charlotte and baby Ru – flew to Exeter in order to go to her funeral. There followed her requiem mass in London in the autumn. These were all family obligations that I could not avoid. Even so, there were one or two people who thought that I should have been immersed so fully in the past that these things would have passed me by.

When I add up the number of nights that I was away from home over the course of the whole year, the total is not so great. It amounts to about twenty, some of which were simply spent at Ram and Charlotte's house when I had gone to town by bus. My trips were spread out over the year, and included a weekend in Galloway for the Reforesting Scotland Gathering, where people were pleased to see me in my petticoats and were keen to know about the particulars of simple living, for it accords with much that the group holds dear. I travelled to the gathering in someone else's car, but there were occasions, dotted throughout the year, when I just had to use my own. By Hogmanay, I found that I had used up exactly two tanks of fuel, some of which had been burnt by Ben and Al, both of whom had borrowed the car. It did not seem a bad record.

The year had broken my dependence on four wheels. I had a look at how much diesel I consumed in 2004 before the whole project started: I used to fill up my tank every two weeks. Afterwards, I decided to give myself an allowance of just half of that. Now, I sternly ask myself whether each journey is really necessary. I also make sure that I have more than a single reason for driving. I give lifts and beg them from my neighbours, too. And during 2006, I filled up only twelve times. That means that I travelled about 7,500 miles by car, using about 143 gallons of diesel. It would have been less, but a work project has taken me on repeated journeys right across the Borders. It would have been almost impossible to get to and fro by means of public transport.

Why is this an issue? Well, the worries that I express in the first chapter about global warming have not gone away: the problem is hammering on the door. The frost-free weeks and gales of January 2007 were almost certainly not just a freak event, any more than the bitterly cold January of 2010. For the world is changing rapidly, and carbon-dioxide emissions – a direct result of our affluent lifestyles – are chasing the thermometer relentlessly upwards. Our weather patterns become ever more unpredictable than they used to be. And we are not at all clear whether we in Britain will freeze or fry. If you want to be convinced, see Al Gore's book (or his film) *An Inconvenient Truth* (2006). Melting icecaps, desiccating land, ocean currents under threat – it is all laid out graphically. The scientists give us just a few years in which to act. It will take government action to force real change, but in order to convince governments that they have a mandate to bring in difficult measures, it seems important to me to get ahead of the game. And to convince others that a green life is not only possible, but fun!

Another thing that I have done is to give up flying in aeroplanes. Aviation is a major source of greenhouse gases, which is why that trip to Exeter was the last time that I flew. Yet I don't want to give up travelling. My cottage year brought it forcibly home to me what being restricted to one locality is like: it stagnates the mind. Being able to move around at will is a great boon, yet we take it for granted. The quest for variety is now deeply embedded in our psyches. I certainly feel that I need to see the world, and crave more than a weekly walk to the village. Now, when I want to go to Edinburgh, I do so by bus. When I want to go to London, I jump on a bus and then the train. In the autumn, when I wanted to go to France, I took the train, and then, with some nostalgia, the Channel ferry. Give me the White Cliffs and seagulls screaming, rather than the sterile environment of an airport, any day. The writer and environmentalist George Monbiot would have had me travelling

Our polar icecaps are melting at an alarming rate.

on Eurostar on account of its better fuel performance, but I classed the voyage as part of my holiday, to be enjoyed whilst I still have the option. That said, people use the same argument about flying: 'Let's do it while we can'. It is a dangerous one, since continuing demand for airways is encouraging their proliferation. I shall have to consider the issue more deeply, and maybe make my holiday travelling as low-carbon-emitting as I possibly can.

There are also losses that I have experienced since emerging from the year. One that I identified quickly was physical exercise. I was no longer chopping wood each morning, or carrying baskets of it inside. I was not hauling water across the yard, and found that I seldom walked to the village and back again. Yet a big bowl of porridge in the morning, and those barley bannocks that I learnt to cook, have become entrenched in my way of life. I soon realised that if I ate these things regularly, while taking only a moderate walk, I would grow fat. So a full year ago now, I decided to double my dog-walking time. Instead of half an hour, I aim for an hour and make sure that there is a good stretch of uphill walking included in our route. (That's not difficult around here, where I can climb a different hill every day.) As a result of this simple measure, I am fitter, and, miraculously, my arthritic dog is less stiff. I am amazed by people who can drag themselves to a gym to work out on horrible equipment in a boring environment – it must be so difficult for them to make themselves keep it up. Yet I can see that modern life, and especially the way that work is organised, forces choices on people that oblige them to go to these strange lengths to keep even moderately fit.

Cycling seems a better option. I enjoy being out on my bike, and being in contact with the world in a manner that is not possible from behind the windscreen of a car. I even did it a few times during 2005, when I had an urgent letter to post. On one occasion, my sins found me out. I needed a ham bone from the butcher in order to make stock. Ram and Charlotte were due, and I wanted to make a rich soup. Time was short, so instead of putting on trousers, I jumped on to my bike in my skirts, held them up at the handlebars and set off. The journey to the village went smoothly. (It's mostly downhill, so not too much pedalling is involved.) But on the way back with my purchase, my skirts locked in the front wheel, causing me to soar over the handlebars and land inelegantly. Not too much hurt, I was gathering myself up and moving the bike out of the road when Ram and Charlotte themselves drove up in the first car to appear after my spill. I was then frogmarched back to the village and made to try on a cycle helmet, which my kind son then purchased for me. Promises were extracted from me: I would wear head protection, and I would not cycle in skirts again!

My greening efforts go beyond transport. The experience of living in the cottage has made it easier for me to reduce my domestic-energy needs. I have fewer lights on, for instance, and low-energy light bulbs are installed throughout the house. The oil-fired central-heating system is only switched on when I have guests; I have put more insulation into the loft and have had the windows professionally draught-proofed. All this conserves the heat from the kitchen Rayburn. It started life as a multi-fuel cooker, running on coal and wood but was then converted to oil. Guilt finally drove me to get it restored for wood-burning, so I'm back to splitting and barrowing logs. I'm fitter and the kitchen is warmer, and there are solar panels for summer hot water.

Living the life of the eighteenth century has toughened me up, although apart from having to wear more layers when I am sitting writing, I don't force too many discomforts on myself nowadays. I use the washing machine with simple gratitude – washing clothes became more and more of a chore as my experiment wore on. These days, I economise by brushing off mud and sponging away marks, thereby reducing the number of times that I run the machine. No one has complained that I smell. (Maybe they are just being polite, but there were comments made during my cottage year, when the aroma of wood smoke was always in my hair and skirts.)

As far as my diet is concerned, it is not just porridge and bannocks that have stayed with me. I have learnt to use every single thing that I grow, or that the wild can provide, and to buy as little as possible. My purchases still include milk, butter, cheese and bacon. Tinned tomatoes (organic ones, of course) have slipped back into my cooking, but I don't buy exotic vegetables. Even red peppers I only bought when they were in full season. Winter vegetables come from too far away, or else burn up fossil fuels in Dutch greenhouses. Instead, I take pleasure in measuring my food's journey in feet, rather than miles. If I buy meat or fish, it is local. And I go on eating really well.

As for state-of-the-art modernity, I scarcely use a mobile phone, much less one with a camera and video facility. I have never had a television, so plasma screens that take up half of the wall pass me by. But I do love my new laptop computer that the boys so kindly bought me as a 'coming-out' present. It's also great to have broadband. Yet I find that the internet is mostly useful for obtaining straightforward facts, and that when I am researching anything and need more depth and incidental knowledge, I turn to books – sometimes ones acquired over the internet, it's true, but many that are from my own shelves. Indeed, my library of books that are devoted to the everyday life of the past goes on growing. I shall never be an expert on domestic history, but my practical experience of trying to live as though it were the 1790s has given me a few insights into the past that people want to share. And as I talk to them, I cannot help but think that many of them have half an eye on the future, as well as on the past. Society as we know it may not be about to collapse, but it no longer feels wholly secure.

As for the cottage, that now seems dreary and unbelievably cold. I show the odd visitor around, and am then thankful to leave and lock the door behind me. I'm reminded of the moment, last thing on a winter evening, when I would cross the yard to evict the cat from the house kitchen. He used to protest, and would turn to stare at me when I locked myself out to join him in the dark and the cold. I had to move fast to prevent him from slipping ahead in an attempt to share the rudimentary comforts of my cottage hearth and lumpy bed. I never did cheat by retreating to my house bedroom, but in the sleet and the gales, the irony of treating myself like the cat made me chuckle ruefully.

Was it worthwhile? Absolutely! I made myself live as simply as people have lived throughout the centuries, and as the majority of people in the world still live. I have conquered a few of the basic skills that are needed in order to do so, have gained some perspective on contemporary life, and have found the inspiration to grow greener. But all the same, as the winter winds batter us again, I'm glad that the experiment is over.

ڸ A Practical Review of the Year ڸ

Whilst I was preparing to enter the cottage, I kept records of everything I planned to bring to the cottage and of the items I bought and made in advance; I also kept notes of my expenditure throughout the year, as well as the various gifts that were brought by visitors. Inevitably, perhaps, these records were dominated by how I fed myself and my guests.

I had to labour to feed myself under several severe constraints. The primary one was the open fire, which offered me the options of using a cooking pot, frying pan or girdle, but not an oven. The range did, in fact, have an oven. Had it retained all of its system of dampers and air controls, and had I fired it with coal, I am sure that I could have baked in it. As it was, in its damaged state, and with wood as a fuel, the oven's only use was for keeping things warm. Still, I was grateful for that, especially when cooking for a large number of people.

The other major constraint was the actual foodstuffs. I gathered and grew things, but bought very few. In the garden, I confined myself not merely to what I could grow, but to what would conceivably have been grown by a determined gardener of the period I adopted. That involved looking at seed catalogues and recipe books to see what foodstuffs were around at the time. My decision not to keep a goat forced me to buy dairy products. Milk, butter and cheese had to be fetched from Innerleithen, the round trip of more than 5 miles to which I refer frequently in my account. My budget was tight, so I confined luxury purchases to the odd lemon and an occasional half-pound of bacon, buying replacements for my collection of spices as I needed them. I once bought a kipper, as this seemed a plausible late-eighteenth-century product, and also received a few as gifts from visitors. Meat just seemed to come my way as frequently as I needed it. Perhaps that worked out as about once a week. My son shot pheasants, and more appeared in the hands of a local poacher, or were left at my door, as were rabbits on a couple of occasions. Venison arrived twice, still warm, from the Wildwood Environmental Project, a forestry conservation group that aims to restore the native woodland species, of which I have long been a part. We are obliged to cull the over-numerous roe deer during the period in which we are establishing young trees. Our project officer was kind enough to see that I received these two animals, both young, knowing that I would be able to butcher them myself, and that I would make good use of them (see page 89).

I enjoyed growing tomatoes again after a year without them!

The final constraint was cooking dishes that have an eighteenth-century pedigree. Many recipes that are thought of as being 'traditional' were greatly modified during the nineteenth century. The bere bannocks that are widely sold in Orkney, for example, are stuffed full (overfull, in my opinion) with bicarbonate of soda, an industrial product that was unknown in 1790. Drop scones and pancakes, those other traditional favourites, were only leavened with baking powder from the mid-nineteenth century on. Baking powder was invented by Alfred Bird, of Bird's custard fame, in 1843, and was much used by the army in the baking of fresh bread for the troops. Both bannocks and pancakes existed before the artificial leavening came in. The flatbread version of bannocks (a recipe for these is given by Marian McNeill in her celebrated book *The Scots Kitchen*) are, to my taste, better than the soda version. I am not so sure about drop scones, though. It is hard to cook them without them becoming leathery, and I have to admit to a little cheating on this score: unexpected visitors were frequently treated to drop scones made with beremeal, milk and egg, with a tiny amount of sugar and a sly teaspoonful of bicarbonate of soda.

Cooking techniques that do have the ring of authenticity as part of a long-established Scottish cuisine are 'stoving' vegetables (from the French, *étuver*, 'to sweat'), long boiling, especially of soups with barley in them, and frying in oatmeal. Used carefully, these cooking methods allowed me to do most of what I wanted.

ᘀ My Nutrition and Food Records ᘀ

Meal of one sort or another was the mainstay of life for everyone in the past, at least before the potato took over half of its role as staple crop. My mind is still boggled by the sheer volume of meal that was deemed necessary for survival. When handed out as part of a wage or stipend, meal was measured by the boll (the equivalent of 140 lb). In the most generous accounts that I have seen, 1 boll per year was a child's ration; 4 bolls was a woman's; while 6 bolls was a man's. That is a prodigious quantity. I was using, at most, 2 oz of oatmeal for porridge and 4 oz of beremeal for bannocks each day. Another 2 oz of oats or barley might have gone into my broth, making a total from these staples of barely 8 oz in weight. That adds up to a mere 183 lb, or 1⅓ boll, over the entire year. If people were finding it necessary to eat three or four times as much starchy food every day to survive, this points to the paucity of other foodstuffs available to them.

These calculations prompted me to work out the energy value of what I was eating. My daily consumption of oats and bere (barley) came to about 800 calories. If I was also eating a good helping of potatoes, that might have given me another 200 calories. The rest I needed came from the smallish amounts of milk, butter and cheese I consumed, which added up to around another 200 calories on ordinary days – more if visitors brought extras – and from vegetables, as well as fruits when they were in season. It looks as though my daily intake was well under 2,000 calories, and was often not much more than 1,500. Perhaps that is why I ended up much thinner by the end of the year, for the UK's recommended level for women is 1,940 calories a day. A woman eating her way through 4 bolls of meal in the past would have been consuming at least 2,400 calories a day (depending on the balance of oats and barley), without counting any extras, such as milk, cheese, butter, other animal fats, eggs, kail, onions and the very occasional bit of meat or fish. You have to work hard all day to burn up 2,400 or more calories, and all of the evidence suggests that people did. I can think of no pictures of fat people dating from that time. As for a man who might have consumed 6 bolls of meal in a year – a stupendous 840 lb, or nearly 2½ lb a day – I do not think that he existed. What's more, I am sure that this ration for men must have incorporated an allowance for growing children who ate more than their 1 boll allocation, and maybe also for visitors, dogs and perhaps even poultry.

Before the year started, I bought in supplies of the different types of meal that I needed. This imitated the part of a schoolmaster's stipend that would have been given in kind. Even the water-driven, stone-ground, organic mill at Golspie in Sutherland works in metric measurements rather than in the imperial measures that were exclusively used in the past. I initially ordered three sacks of meal weighing 25 kg each, or a boll and a bit (3 x 25 kg = 75 kg = 165 lb). Judging by the calculations that I had just done, this seemed an uncannily accurate amount for my personal consumption, but in reality was not enough, for I was feeding far more mouths than merely my own. Thankfully, Innes Miller, a kind friend who travels regularly to Caithness, passing right by the door of the Golspie mill, brought reinforcements. In the end, I got through more than two sacks of beremeal and nearly two of pinhead oatmeal, but the medium-oatmeal sack was not finished. (The tail end of it, infested by insects, ended up being fed to some chicks, but not until a full two years after it was purchased.)

My Supply of Meal for the Year

oatmeal (pinhead, medium and fine): 150 lb
beremeal: 110 lb
peasemeal: a small quantity

Vegetables from the Garden

onions
spinach
leeks
marrows
  (two types)
garlic
lettuce
  (three types)
parsnips
rocket
carrots
peas
neeps

marrowfat peas
  for drying
white turnips
beans for drying
kail (two types)
radishes
cabbage
  (three types)
cucumbers
broad beans
beetroot
green beans
potatoes
  (six varieties)

Herbs from the Garden

thyme
caraway
marjoram
chamomile
mint
fennel
sage
dill
chives

Fruits & Nuts from the Garden

rhubarb
apples
  (ten varieties)
strawberries
pears
  (two varieties)
gooseberries
plums
  (three varieties)
raspberries
hazelnuts
blackcurrants
redcurrants

WILD FOOD

nettles
wild garlic
wild marjoram
sorrel
bishop's weed
hedge garlic
  for salads
hawthorn
  for salads

hazelnuts
blaeberries
wild raspberries
brambles
elderflowers
elderberries
crabapples

Meat & Fish from the Back Yard or the Wild

pheasants:
  about ten
salmon: one
rabbits:
  about eight
trout: ten
hare: one

chicken: two
venison: two
  small deer
eggs: 1/2 dozen
  a week
wild boar:
  two chops

ITEMS BOUGHT

cheddar: 1/2 lb a week
milk: 4 pt a week
butter: 1/2 lb
a fortnight
bacon: 1/2 lb a month
lemons: about one a
  week on average
sugar: 8 lb over the year
  (mostly for wine)

cinnamon, nutmeg, ginger,
  mace: small quantities
groats (whole, husked
  oats): 4 lb
pot barley: 8 lb
two rabbits for my
  birthday meal

two large haggis for
  Burns Night
one kipper
salt herring for
  Christmas Eve

Items Provided over the Year by Visiting Friends

six kippers
ten trout
two mackerel
two smoked trout
one Arbroath smokie
8 lb honey (some in
  exchange for eggs)
seven loaves
3 lb cheese
1/2 pt double cream

three pots chutney
five pots jam
one pot ginger balls
  in syrup
four rabbits
three pheasants
two wild-boar chops
several joints venison
one side Parma ham
five cakes

two boxes cocoa
oranges
lemons
one pineapple
numerous bottles win
one bottle homemade
  mead (very good!)
one bottle Madeira

SEASONAL MENUS

I ate porridge, brose, bannocks, oatcakes and potatoes, whether new or from store, throughout the year, along with dried foods that I had prepared the previous year, but most of my food was seasonal.

SPRING:
Nettle soup (page 71)
Sorrel soup (page 71)
Wild-garlic paste (page 73)
Spinage with eggs (page 79)
Stovies and other potato dishes
Root vegetable dishes
Dried pea and bean dishes
Wild salads
Rocket from cold frame
Purple sprouting broccoli
Rhubarb
Dried apple rings & prunes

SUMMER:
Meagre broth (page 65)
Spinach soup (similar to sorrel
  soup, see page 71)
Hotchpotch (page 54)
Trout cooked in clay (page 127)
Stewed 'rabbets' (page 81)
Eggs
Peas & broad beans
Lightly stoved (or stir-fried)
  summer vegetables
Groats
New potatoes
Beetroots
Runner beans
Prune pudding (page 81)
Blackcurrant keesel (page 132)
Cranachan (page 141)
Salads
Soft fruits
plums

AUTUMN:
Leek & oatmeal soup (page 168)
Game soup (page 167)
Boiled pheasants (page 165)
Scotch pheasants (page 165)
Stoved root vegetables (page 54)
Parsnip dishes
Leek dishes
Beetroots
Marrows (pumpkins & squashes)
Potato dishes
Brambles & blaeberries
Apples & pears
Eggs

WINTER
Scotch broth (page 171)
Cockyleekie (page 170)
Rumbledethumps (page 53)
Pease pottage (page 136)
Venison sokey (page 195)
Root vegetable dishes
Cabbage dishes
Red cabbage dishes
Leek dishes
Potato dishes
Mixed vegetable stews
  with dried beans
Neeps
Baked apples
Oatmeal pudding
Prunes

৶ What it all Cost ৶

GROCERIES

Dairy products	£ 267
Bacon	£ 25
Bacon shanks for broth	£ 10
Haggis	£ 9.50
Kippers	£ 12
Sugar (jam and wine-making)	£ 14.50
Honey	£ 22.62
Salt	£ 2
Pot barley	£ 6.18
Dried peas	£ 1.06
Dried beans	£ 3.48
Tea	£ 8.78
Coffee	£ 5.36
Lemons	£ 10
Apples	£ 35
Total groceries	£ 432.48
(£8 a week on average)	

MEAL

Bere meal: 1 sack	£ 45.99
Oatmeal: 1 sack	£ 32.13
Peasemeal	£ 3.06
Total meal	£ 81.18

(meal would have been given as part of a schoolmaster's stipend)

GRAIN FOR HENS £ 25

SEEDS FOR SOWING

Basic vegetable	£ 44.25
Heritage varieties	£ 18.95
Total vegetable seeds	£ 63.20

HOUSEHOLD

8 boxes x 50 candles	£ 24
(the rest were homemade)	
soap	£ 5
Total household	£ 29.00

DRESS

Muslin	£ 6.90
Lawn	£ 39.90
Cheesecloth for clouts	£ 11.64
Broderie anglaise	£ 12.00
Shoes	£ 120
(clogs & Moroccan mules)	
Total dress	£ 190.44

WRITING PAPER £ 29

STAMPS £ 183.60

BUS TRAVEL £ 235.50

(average of one trip per fortnight)

GRAND TOTAL £1274.40

Average cost of living per week:
£ 24.50

Estimated funds available to 1790s schoolmaster: £20 per annum (Sterling), which translates into approximately £1300 in contemporary money, i.e. £25 per week.

❧ ADDENDA ❧
Glossary, Index,
Bibliography &c.

ℒ GLOSSARY ℒ

Arbroath smokie *a lightly smoked haddock, speciality of Arbroath*
baffled (entrance) *partitioned, to prevent cold air from entering*
barm *a natural yeast, created by allowing a mixture of flour and water to ferment*
barmkin *a defensive wall around a tower house, found in Scotland and Northern England*
bere/bear *a primitive variety of barley grown in Scotland*
beremeal *a whole-grain flour milled from bere*
besom *a traditional broom made from twigs tied onto a pole*
blaeberry *small, dark-blue berry (known in England as a bilberry)*
boll *an old measurement of oats, equal to 6 bushels*
brash *pile of rubbish, such as hedge clippings*
braxy *an animal, usually sheep, that died of natural causes*
brose *porridge made by stirring boiling liquid into oatmeal or any other type of meal*
bucht *an enclosure for milking sheep*
burn *a small stream*
cailleach/Cailleach *an old woman; the Spirit of Winter*
catch *a round, often sung in such a way as to sound ridiculous*
ceilidh *a party with traditional Scottish music, dancing, and storytelling*
chessit *a cheese-press*
choppin *an old measurement, nearly an English quart*
cleuch *a narrow, wooded glen*
clouts *a piece of cloth used for household cleaning*
collop *an escalope, or small cutlet of meat*
cran *an old fishing basket, originally used to measure the herring catch*
cranachan *a traditional Scottish dessert, using cream, whisky, oats and (usually) fruit*
creel *a wicker basket for carrying fish, usually carried on the back*
crottle *a type of lichen, used to make reddish-brown or purple dye*
crusie *a small open lamp, in which the pith of rushes is burned in animal fat*

curds *the part of milk that thickens when milk sours or is treated with enzymes*

dockens *docks, the weed that often grows near nettles*

dominie *a Scottish schoolmaster*

dreich *dreary, damp weather*

drove *road an old track once used to drive livestock from the Highlands to markets to the south*

drystane *a building contructed by fitting together stones without mortar*

farles *the quarter segments of an oatcake or bannock*

fermtoun *a group of cottages clustered around the land the people worked*

gean *wild cherry*

girdle *a circular iron plate used for baking oatcakes and scones*

groats *whole-grain oats that have been dried and then crushed*

grozets *gooseberries*

gudebread *raisin bannocks, scones, etc.; traditionally baked for weddings and other family celebrations*

guid *Scots 'good'*

guid·wife *the mistress of the house*

guising *going about in disguise, costume*

[hay] heck *hay rack for cattle*

herd [tender of lifestock] *a shepherd*

heritor *richer landowners in a parish, responsible for funding public services*

inby *inner fields, those nearest to the farmhouse*

jaunting car *light two-wheeled horse-drawn carriage, popular in Ireland*

kebbock *a whole wheel of cheese*

kirk *church*

kist *a large storage chest or box*

lum *a chimney; a hanging lum is a type of hood placed over a fire to direct smoke up the chimney*

manse *a minister's official residence*

mantua *a loose-fitting gown popular in the 17th and 18th centuries*

mart *a cow or ox that is fattened and killed to provide meat for the winter*

mashlum *flour with different types of grain mixed together*

meith *a boundary marker*

mutch *a lightweight bonnet, tied beneath the chin*

neeps *turnips*

palliasse *a straw mattress*

pancheon *a large bowl used for liquids, often for washing*

pease/peasemeal *peas/meal made from peas*

peel/pele tower *a small defensive tower, common in the Borders*

pigs [storage jars] *earthenware storage jars*

plenishings *furniture and household effects*

policies [woodland] *the grounds of a country estate, hence 'policy woodland'*

pot herb *green vegetable for cooking*

pottage *a thick soup or porridge*

proddy rug *a rag rug, made by pushing scraps of material through a cloth with a wooden spike*

riggs *sections of a ploughed field*

runrig *ridges, from a field in which the alternate ridges belong to different owners*

sark *a loose-fitting dress or shift, worn beneath outer clothes*

scrip *a leather bag or satchel*

sheiling *a hut used by shepherds for temporary accommodation*

shor goun *short, jacket-like garment worn by women in the 18th and 19th centuries*

spill *a small twist of paper or slip of wood used to light a fire*

spinage *spinach*

spit *a skewer for roasting meat or vegetables over a fire*

spunk *an old-fashioned match, tipped with sulfur and used to light the fire*

stovie *dish of sliced potatoes, cooked in water and fat*

tirling pin *a door-knocker, consisting of an iron ring and serrated rod; the ring was rattled up and down the rod to make a noise*

whins *gorse or furze*

whinstone *dark-coloured, fine-grained rocks, such as basalt (or flint)*

FURTHER READING

This list by no means collects everything that I read but tries instead
to include what was most useful or interesting. Not everything is in
print, but if you want an overview that is, try Maisie Steven's book.
It is an excellent introduction to the wonderful resource that is
the 'First Statistical Accounts'. Anyone wishing to know more about
their own parish should go to the real thing, which is available either
in Scotland's larger libraries or online:
    http: www//stat-acc-scot.edina.ac.uk/sas

First-hand accounts

Elizabeth Grant of Rothiemurchus, _Memoirs of a Highland Lady_,
    Canongate, 1988.

Dorothy Wordsworth, _Recollections of a Tour made in Scotland_, Yale
    University Press, 1997.

John Galt, _Annals of the Parish_, Mercat Press, 1994 (fiction, but of
    the period).

General books

Maisie Steven, _Parish Life in Eighteenth-Century Scotland_, Scottish
    Cultural Press 2002.

Marjorie Plant, _The Domestic Life of Scotland in the Eighteenth Century_,
    Edinburgh University Press, 1952.

I. F. Grant, _Highland Folk Ways_, Routledge, Kegan & Paul, 1975.

Food

F. Marian McNeill, _The Scots Kitchen_, Mercat Press, 2004.

Elizabeth Cleland, _New and Easy Method of Cookery_, 1755.

Annette Hope, _A Caledonian Feast_, Canongate, 2002.

Catherine Brown, _Feeding Scotland_, National Museums of Scotland, 1994.

Felicity Lawrence, _Not on the Label_, Penguin Books, 2004.

Plants

William Milliken and Sam Bridgewater, _Flora Celtica_, Birlinn, 2004.

Tess Darwin, _The Scots Herbal_, Mercat Press, 2006.

ACKNOWLEDGEMENTS

So many people helped me to sustain the year with their enthusiasm and practical contributions that it is hard to remember all of them. What I do recall is how generous everyone was in entering into the spirit of the enterprise.

I must first thank Patrick Cave-Browne for taking my project so seriously and for making sure that I had all the technology, and its mastery, that I needed for the project. His regular visits with his wife, Mary (the generous donor of lovely objects like a fine horn scoop and the ancient Pashmina), were enormously helpful. Secondly, John Behm has my grateful thanks for the hard labour and lovely workmanship that he put into the cottage renovation. His visits with his wife, Rachael, and little son, Mungo, were always fun and I will not forget that he met my need for music by sitting in the cottage and singing to me, even though his face was battered and bruised from a nasty car accident.

Next I must thank all of my neighbours and friends for putting up with having a time-traveller in their midst, and for their cups of coffee and warm firesides when I sought refuge from the cold past! They genuinely contributed to my welfare on many accounts, especially Peter Lee, who allowed me to barrow away his entire stock of gash timber to burn on my fire, and Brian Malcolm, who was always dropping off a sack of kindling. Friends Ann & Bill Goodburn were also kind enough to bring firewood whenever they visited. It was another friend, Helen Douglas, who guessed that I would appreciate evening visits. She was the only person who regularly turned up after dark, often bearing honey, which was always a treat. Another friend, Innes Miller, played a vital role. He was my carter, carrying meal all the way from Sutherland (where he goes regularly) and kindly bringing it the extra thirty miles from Edinburgh to the Borders. In addition, there were many, many kind people who went out of their way to visit me: it was their sociability that really kept me going.

There are also thanks due to four more people for practical, as well as moral, support. One is Sam Wade, who sorted out so many minor problems for me, from mending my copper kettle to making the door latch properly. Another is Charlie Poulsen, who was ready for any task that needed an extra pair of hands. The third is Martin Murphy, who came in the year following my experiment and sorted out several structural problems in the main house, some of which had been caused by my neglect of the fabric during my year in the cottage. Lastly there is Liz Findlay, who made special visits to take some most useful photographs.

Finally I would like to thank my family, especially Ram & Charlotte, Ben & Cal, and Gaie & Toby for putting up with my eccentricities and for all the love, practical help and support that they gave me, from nailing up lining boards in the rush to finish the cottage, to overseeing the party arrangements when I was about to leave it. This list would not be complete without mentioning Stephanie Wolfe-Murray, who encouraged me to seek a publisher and who volunteered to copy-edit my text. Last of all, I must thank Sara Hunt and her team for thinking that this book was worth publishing in such a lavish form and for expending such energy and enthusiasm on its creation.

F.J.H. Innerleithen, December 2008

The publisher would like to thank the following people for their assistance in the creation of this book: Clare Melinsky; John O'Neill, Nick Hayes and others who took photographs especially for the book (see the credits below); Sara Myers, for the glossary and more; Ron Grosset; Liz Small; Peter Murray; Chris McCartney; Bill and Kath Mulvey; Geoffrey Blackwell.

PHOTO AND ILLUSTRATION CREDITS

INDEX